4.80

THE INEQUALITY
OF STATES

Oxford University Press, Ely House, London W.1

GLASGOW NEW YORK TORONTO MELBOURNE WELLINGTON
CAPE TOWN SALISBURY IBADAN LUSAKA ADDIS ABABA
BOMBAY CALCUTTA MADRAS KARACHI LAHORE DACCA
KUALA LUMPUR HONG KONG TOKYO

THE INEQUALITY
OF STATES

A Study of the Small Power
in International Relations

BY

DAVID VITAL

CLARENDON PRESS · OXFORD
1967

© *Oxford University Press* *1967*

PRINTED AND BOUND IN ENGLAND BY
HAZELL WATSON AND VINEY LTD
AYLESBURY, BUCKS

To the memory of
my father
MEIR GROSSMAN

ACKNOWLEDGEMENTS

I SHOULD like to record a particular debt of gratitude to Professor Max Beloff of All Souls College, Oxford, and Mr. James Joll, Sub-Warden of St. Antony's College, Oxford, for their advice and warm encouragement during the preparation of this study. I have also had the benefit of valuable comments from Professor Geoffrey Goodwin of the London School of Economics and Political Science, Professor Agnes Headlam-Morley of the University of Oxford, my colleague Miss Elizabeth Hopkins of the University of Sussex, and Mr. E. F. Jackson of the University of Oxford. I must also thank the Warden and Fellows of St. Antony's College, Oxford, for their hospitality to me during the year 1965–6, as well as the Librarian of St. Antony's for her help and courtesy. Lastly I must thank my Head of Department in the Israel Government Service for having agreed to my taking leave of absence for the period in which the book was being written and prepared for publication. Responsibility for the contents of this study is, of course, entirely my own and in no way reflects the views of any official or academic body to which I have belonged. I should also state clearly that the factual material which has been used to support and elucidate the argument was drawn exclusively from published sources.

D. V.

University of Sussex,
Falmer, Brighton

March 1967

CONTENTS

CONTENTS

PART I

DISABILITIES

INTRODUCTION

Th is study is an attempt to spell out some of the practical political implications of the material inequality of states. While the formal equality of states is a valuable and, on the whole, valued convention of international relations it is evident that in peace, no less than in war, differences of size have political consequences for both large and small nations. All things being equal, the state with great economic resources and a large population has more influence on events outside its frontiers, greater security from pressure and attack, more prestige, and a larger element of choice in respect of the national policy it pursues. A small state is more vulnerable to pressure, more likely to give way under stress, more limited in respect of the political options open to it and subject to a tighter connexion between domestic and external affairs. In other words the smaller the human and material resources of a state the greater are the difficulties it must surmount if it is to maintain any valid political options at all and, in consequence, the smaller the state the less viable it is as a genuinely independent member of the international community. Of course, sheer physical (human and material) size is not the only factor. The level of economic and social development that has been attained, the chance effects of geographical proximity to areas of conflict and importance between and to the great powers, the nature of the environment in which the state is placed, the cohesion of the population and the degree of internal support given the government of the day—these are some of the factors that modify the ability of the state to perform as a resistant rather than vulnerable, and active rather than passive, member of the international community. But material size is the factor which is least of all given to modification through the deliberate efforts of governments. It sets the limit to what can be attained and fixes the international role and status of the nation more securely than any other.

Since the Second World War the economic and military power available to the great states has vastly increased. It is true that for reasons which are beyond the scope of this book, but of which the most important are the acquisition of nuclear power and the strategic deadlock that has ensued, the great powers have been reluctant to employ their power to the full. Some very great states have, in effect, abdicated from positions of influence; in other cases there is uncertainty as to whether and how available power can be safely and effectively exploited in the national interest. One consequence of this has been that the post-war proliferation of small states has occurred in an atmosphere peculiarly conducive to illusions about national strength and to a corresponding emphasis and reliance on the formal, *legal*, equality of nations. This may be a good or a bad thing; what is uncertain is whether it will last. But the fact that great states have, from time to time, broken through their inhibitions to exert some part at least of the vast economic and military power available to them in order to impose their will on others suggests that reliance on these inhibitions would be misplaced and that the operative factors in crisis remain the national interest as seen at the time and the material bars, if any, to its pursuit.

The strength and weakness of states and their longterm viability must therefore be examined not in terms of current, typical international practice, still less in terms of legal and moral rights. It is the capacity of the state to withstand stress, on the one hand, and its ability to pursue a policy of its own devising, on the other, that are the key criteria. And these can best be explored in terms of limiting cases, exposed positions and barriers which cannot, possibly, be surmounted.

In alternative terms, this study attempts to answer three questions:

(a) What are the practical consequences for the small power of the material inequality of states?

(b) What are the limits of the small power's strength and, in particular, its capacity to withstand great external stresses?

(c) Given its limited resources and the ease with which overwhelming strength can be marshalled against it, what national policies are open to the small power to pursue?

Of course, some small powers can—and in very many cases do—seek to offset their weaknesses by association or alliance with other powers, great and small. But where the quest for protection and insurance is successful a price must normally be paid in terms of sacrifice of autonomy in the control of national resources and loss of freedom of political manoeuvre and choice. For such states the answers to the first and third questions posed above are largely predetermined. As for the second question, the task of unravelling what fraction or aspect of national power[1] it owes to its own resources and what to its partners, apart from being extremely complex in itself, would teach little about the general problems of the small state as an independent international entity. Furthermore, it is only when acting alone— rather than in concert with other, greater states—that the small power can be said to be pursuing an external policy which is in any sense of a class with the external policies of great powers and capable of being compared with them. And it is only when the small power is unaligned and unprotected that the full implications of, say, maintaining or failing to maintain a modern defence establishment can be seen. In short, it is when the state is *alone*—not necessarily in all its affairs, but at least in the great and crucial ones—and is thrown back on its own resources that the limitations and, indeed, the possibilities inherent in its condition are best seen.

---

[1] In the sense that 'political power is a psychological relation between those who exercise it and those over whom it is exercised'. Hans J. Morgenthau, *Politics Among Nations*, 3rd edition, New York, 1962, p. 29.

Nevertheless, if the rough limits of the isolated small power's strength can be delineated and its characteristic disabilities outlined, something that is typical of all small states will have been shown. For the unaligned state can best be regarded as a limiting case for the class of small states, one from which all other small states shade off in varying and progressively lessening degrees of political and military isolation. What can be said of the limiting case is likely to be applicable *mutatis mutandis* to the others. It is of the unaligned power as the paradigm for all small powers that the present study is conceived.

For this reason the present attempt at an analysis of the political viability of the small state has been cast in terms of the isolated, maverick, unaligned power, the small power *alone*—the state which can rely least on outside help and sympathy and which, by virtue of its situation, is compelled to make its own decisions on the basis of its own understanding of that situation and such resources as are available to it.

There is no simple term which adequately expresses this condition. The one used most frequently here—'non-alignment'—is not entirely satisfactory because it has special political, not to mention emotive, connotations. But I have found none better. At any rate, it is used here in its simplest sense, the negative one of implying that there are no clear, effective and mutually binding ties with other powers. Nothing of the legal or ideological significance that attaches to such terms as 'neutrality' and 'neutralism' is intended. The test of 'non-alignment' is seen as whether the state in question must rely ultimately on its own political and material resources in the pursuit of an external policy of its own devising—or not. In consequence, a formal commitment which is ignored in practice, or which has fallen into desuetude, or which has been explicitly or implicitly denounced will be given no weight. It is the actual state of political affairs which is thought to matter, not the legal one. And it follows that such formal obligations as, say, France bore towards Czechoslovakia in 1938 or which the members of the Arab League bear towards each other today are not taken as invalidating an *ex post facto* view of Czechoslovakia then and a contemporary view of Egypt or Syria now as *unaligned* states in substantially the same sense that Sweden and Burma are of this category, whatever differences there may be on historical and other scores.

Some clarification on the term 'small state'[1] is clearly necessary, but there is the difficulty that if an objective definition is attempted it will be circular: along the lines of 'those powers which lack/possess the resources and ability to maintain an independent international role are true small powers, those that do/do not are pseudo small powers' when it is the intention of this study to explore the circumstances under which a small state can maintain such a role. A frankly subjective, if not arbitrary definition has therefore been chosen. But it is one which is supported by common usage.

We recognize, or find it convenient to posit, that the world community is divided into certain, admittedly loose, groups. The formal equality of states notwithstanding, these groups have from time to time been given a degree of overt and even legal recognition.[2] The fundamental test has almost invariably been that of actual or potential military power, modified, to be sure, by historical and contemporary political circumstances. However, it is only the top of the pyramid that is normally defined with any clarity, while it is important to distinguish between at least two more broad classes among the lesser states. Some of these, while outside the generally accepted category of great powers, are nevertheless so populous (Indonesia and Pakistan, for example)

---

[1] 'State' and 'power' are used throughout as interchangeable terms.

[2] At the Paris Peace Conference (1919) 'Great Powers' were entitled to five delegates, 'Lesser Powers' to three, 'New States' to two, 'States in process of formation' to one and 'Neutrals' to one. The League of Nations and the United Nations have perpetuated (and somewhat modified) this tradition, which may be said to have been formally initiated for the modern period at the Congress of Vienna.

that their cases cannot reasonably be compared with those of their small neighbours (say, Malaysia and Ceylon). Similarly, certain less heavy populated, but more highly developed states (such as Argentina, Canada and Poland) are properly distinguished from smaller states of a roughly equivalent level of development (such as Uruguay and Finland). The present study is concerned with the latter class of smaller states to the exclusion of such middle powers. The dividing line between the two groups may be drawn by defining the rough upper limits of the class of small states as being:

(*a*) a population of 10–15 million in the case of economically advanced countries; and

(*b*) a population of 20–30 million in the case of underdeveloped countries.

The first group would therefore include Sweden, Australia, Belgium and Switzerland, for example, but not Italy; the second group would include most of the South and Central American states, but not Mexico or Brazil, all the Arab states and all the African states except Nigeria.[1]

This is, of necessity, very imperfect. Certainly, no pretence is made that the 2:1 relationship between developed and under-developed populations is anything but rough and convenient. It has been argued by some economists that the term 'under-developed' is excessively crude in any case. But while this point is important to economists concerned with the origins of under-development and its cure, here the interest is solely with the brute fact of under-development and its general, but nevertheless plain, limiting effect on military and economic potential.

No lower limit has been set: it seems evident that the disabilities that are a consequence of size where the population is ten million will clearly be intensified where it is five or ten times smaller. However, such 'micro-powers' as Western Samoa have not been seriously considered at all. They surely

---

[1] At the time of writing the future of Nigeria as a great federal state is unclear.

constitute yet another class of states with reasonably distinct and characteristic problems of their own.

Finally, it should, perhaps, be stressed that these definitions are put forward to make clear the identity of the subject of this study, not with a view to the creation of a precise concept for manipulative analytical purposes.

MENTAL AND ADMINISTRATIVE
PERSPECTIVES

I

I T is a commonplace of political behaviour that in the minds of leaders facts tend to arrange themselves around purposes. In domestic politics the purposes striven for are reasonably clear: broadly speaking, the acquisition and retention of power. They are, moreover, easily definable in advance of any consideration of circumstances and of the observed facts of the situation that presents itself to the leaders and to their subordinates in the hierarchies of party and government. Indeed, the nature and significance of the 'facts' are determined to a substantial degree by the political purposes of those who select them at any given level in the hierarchies. It is the purposes that guide the selection of data, that give them relevance and meaning and that largely determine the level of generalization at which they will be employed in analysis and policy formulation. Along the finely shaded spectrum of ever greater generalization that leads from what may be termed the atomic social datum to the political symbol or image, the tendency is to operate at a point nearer to the latter limit than to the former. And this pre-supposes a measure of transformation whereby the data are ordered, combined and adjusted for serious use. It has indeed been argued with considerable force that

Often the environment is effective only through the mediation of symbols. Especially is this true in the case of political action where the environment is both spatially and logically distant.[1]

[1] Harold D. Lasswell and Abraham Kaplan, *Power and Society*, New Haven, 1957, p. 26.

What is, at the very least, a strong tendency in domestic affairs becomes, in international relations, an inescapable and necessary process. This is by no means simply a function of the requirements of *raison d'état* and the rigid framework of thought and observation that it imposes. It would seem to arise out of the extraordinary complexity of international affairs and the unique difficulty of deciding which aspects of them are to be taken as significant for the purpose in hand and which can be safely ignored. Some of the reasons for this pertain to the nature of the 'environment' itself. In the world of states the complexities and uncertainties characteristic of domestic affairs are to be found multiplied and compounded. Each nation is, of course, a unique social and political complex and the ties and similarities between them are less important and instructive than the differences and discontinuities. Each is therefore 'spatially and logically distant' from the foreign observer and therefore generally beyond more than somewhat superficial comprehension by him. Cultural, linguistic and ideological disparities lead to large and unbridgeable gaps in the information collected and the interpretations and assessments offered even by trained and professional observers, let alone by policymakers whose expertise, if any, is likely to be in their own domestic sphere. The walls of secrecy and privilege that surround the activities of governments may not everywhere be of the same density or effectiveness, but there is no administration that is not in some respects and in some degree closed to foreign inquiry. Apart from certain restricted aspects of military, scientific and other technical intelligence, there can thus be no really thorough, let alone complete, knowledge of the affairs of a foreign government—even pre-supposing readiness to indulge in the vast expense and trouble that the attempt to obtain such knowledge would involve.

What is true at the lower, specialist or desk level of foreign and intelligence services is true, *a fortiori*, at the higher, policy-making and policy-proposing level where by custom and necessity the geographical range of concern widens with increased responsibility and authority. At these higher levels, even where officials are wholly or chiefly concerned with foreign topics, attention to the affairs of any *single* country must necessarily be discontinuous and acquaintance with them superficial in due proportion. Alternatively, attention will be largely riveted on countries which are thought of prime importance. But even there only the expert or specialist is in a position to acquire and absorb the detail since the greater the importance ascribed to a given problem the greater will generally be the quantity of data amassed. The consequence is that even where the non-specialist policymaker is prepared to rely upon the expert and be aided by him, he himself is impelled to operate with a group of relatively restricted political symbols, images and generalities within a somewhat inflexible and schematic system of ideas. These symbols and schemata are, indeed, based upon and nourished by the information and ideas provided by the experts. But the policy-maker, if he is to be effective, must construct—or reconstruct—them for himself. It is precisely in his ability to formulate his own view and policy out of the materials supplied by his officials that a strong foreign minister differs from a weak one.

If it were only for this comparatively straightforward, though certainly very important, problem of information and its handling for policy-formulation purposes the difference between the perception and interpretation of the foreign and domestic environments would be largely one of degree. Yet there is clearly a difference of kind as well.

Firstly, there is the fundamental difficulty of determining what are the proper, or at any rate most useful or appropriate subjects for attention. It is a difficulty which goes far beyond the bounds of, say, the professional diplomat's familiar dilemma whether to devote more time to cultivating the party in power or the party in opposition. It concerns a general uncertainty about which factors are directly relevant to the external behaviour of states and which are only marginally so. This uncertainty is at the heart of much of the indecision and argument in western capitals in recent years over the most efficacious policy to adopt towards states which have been judged hostile or recalcitrant at various times—North Viet-Nam, Cuba, Egypt, and South Africa, for example. Assuming the will and ability to apply pressure, what kind of pressure? Economic, diplomatic, military? And of what precise nature? And how much or how little and in what mixture? And at what target and at what juncture? The answers to this kind of question depend in great measure on one's knowledge and understanding of the policy-making processes in the state in question and this in turn is conditional on a great deal of very precise information and a deep insight into that country's affairs. In practice, understanding of requisite validity and profundity is rarely, if ever, attained. Yet practical decisions must be taken despite the obvious imperfection of the materials on which they are—nominally, at least—based. All this reinforces the tendency to employ images in thinking about external affairs and to believe in and rely on the images employed and the schematic relations constructed to connect them with each other. And this, in turn, makes for greater difficulty in inter-state relations and communication than there might otherwise be—there being no reason why the images and constructs familiar to and favoured by the leaders of one state should resemble those favoured by the leaders of another.

Secondly, the purposes of political leaders in their inter-state relations are rarely as clear or as coherent as in their domestic affairs. The fully megalomaniac statesman to whom coherence comes easily is the exception, not the rule. For others there is no real equivalent to the straightforward pursuit of power and office in home politics, at any rate not in the contemporary world. Where that is the *aim*, even in part, it must be sought deviously rather than directly and its attainment will generally be fraught with greater risks of frustration and disaster than any met with in the domestic sphere. So the problem of defining the practical purposes of foreign policy remains. In most countries—though certainly not all—the purposes of foreign policy are in fact either substantially negative (e.g. maintenance of national independence and security), or too general to serve as more than vague indicators of the spirit in which affairs are to be conducted (e.g. enhanced prosperity, economic welfare, prestige), or else left totally undefined. The problem of how to make the transition from such vague, self-evident and platitudinous calls for a satisfactory rather than an unsatisfactory state of affairs to even a very general formulation of policy (such as the post-war American policy of containment) is a difficult one. Policy is distinct from purpose. One refers to what should be done, the other to why. The purposes remain logically and actually distinct from policy both where they can be authoritatively defined—which is rarely the case—and where they can only be set down as part of an elaborate *ex post facto* intellectual exercise. What matters is that since they are rarely clear to those most concerned, even to those who make most play with them, they cannot perform the vital function of fastening the attention of both policy-maker and specialist adviser on those aspects of the international scene which are of direct importance and relevance to them. Only in times of very great danger or of war, when 'survival' or 'victory' are the watchwords, or when some megalomaniac leader's will is paramount in influential thinking, does the machine spring to life and the general sense of clear and unmistakable purpose impel sharp appreciation of the external world and an effective distinction of the relevant from the irrelevant. Otherwise, and in most cases, the business of making order out of the welter of foreign data proceeds in an uncertain and unconvincing fashion—particularly in democratic states—and problems are forever being redefined, issues restated, relationships reappraised and policies reconsidered. This is the case even where these processes are inexplicit or even unconscious.

In this intellectual confusion in which foreign affairs are viewed and foreign relations conducted, the role of general notions, formulae, prejudices, images and symbols is immense and the search for coherence is unending. The force of the generalities is that they make coherence possible. There is, of course, no uniformity about these general ideas or manners of viewing external events. They vary from state to state and from society to society. The individual's private view may be important at a given juncture. But some ideas and some manners of viewing external events are sufficiently common to be generalized in their turn, as are the circumstances that encourage or provoke their use and acceptance. This chapter will therefore consider some of the characteristic ways in which the small power views the international arena and in which it itself is seen, particularly by the great power. But as these perspectives have very little significance in the abstract, the machinery that tends, consciously or unconsciously, to be guided by them—the foreign and intelligence establishments of great and small powers—will first be compared and the link between outlook and apparatus examined.

II

The profession and function of diplomacy is not accorded equal respect or importance in all societies and it would, of course, be absurd to attempt to generalize about the actual contribution of diplomatic machinery—ministries and foreign services—to policy-making in any class of states. Certainly, the prestige and influence of the professional bodies concerned, along with their various ancillary and related agencies, vary with a multitude of factors of which the size of the state is only one. But since 'States will always need to organize their relationships with each other in some way or another,'[1] and this organization exacts a price in high-class manpower and in money, the manner in which these affairs are organized, the quantities of money expended, the numbers of officials involved and, above all, where and in what concentration they are located must de-

[1] Sir William Hayter, *The Diplomacy of the Great Powers*, 1961, p. 74.

pend on what resources are available and at the same time indicate something both significant and characteristic of the external affairs of the state under consideration. At the very least, the geographical dispersal and concentration of diplomatic officials can be seen as an indicator—perhaps crude, but by no means misleading—of where, that is in which capitals, the state's major external interests are thought to lie and what weight is attached to specific areas and subjects. For of the three classic functions of diplomacy—representation, negotiation and intelligence—two, negotiation (employed in the widest sense) and intelligence—require manpower in a proportion that is quantitatively related to the intensity and range with which they are conducted.

Where representation is the principal business of an embassy, an ambassador and perhaps a single secretary will suffice. But where trade, aid, military assistance and procurement, air and navigation agreements, political discussions of a degree of seriousness that is above that of the seasonal *tour d'horizon*, or any of the other myriad tasks a mission may perform are in fact required, then a substantial increase of personnel must follow. It is thus perfectly natural and proper that the Ambassador of Haiti in London be attended by a single diplomatic officer, while the Ambassador of the United States be attended by 114.[1] Also that among these 114 officers there may be representatives of as many as forty different agencies of the American Government over and above those of the State Department proper.[2] The amassing of information on the host country requires manpower no less than the negotiation function; but unlike it, the proportion in which the functionaries concerned will occupy formally diplomatic posts varies very considerably from service to service and from post to post. Still, it is safe to assume that where the collection of intelligence on a given state is thought worthwhile the fact will be duly reflected in the size of the diplomatic mission maintained there.

[1] *Foreign Office List*, 1965.
[2] Arthur M. Schlesinger, Jr., *A Thousand Days*, 1965, p. 369.

It is true that the extent to which missions are inflated by diplomatic and technical personnel clearly depends to some extent on the bureaucratic practices and security inhibitions of the state in question. But while there is no way in which these factors can be accurately measured and their effects compared, it seems fairly reasonable to believe that, on the whole, and with only a few and rather obvious exceptions, they will be less decisive than the factors with which we are directly concerned here, namely where the state's main business lies and what its nature is.

With these generalities in mind, the comparison of some random sets of figures would seem to substantiate what we would, on other grounds, expect to be the case where the foreign establishments of small and great states are compared.

Firstly, the greater states, including the former imperial powers, tend to maintain nearly universal networks of diplomatic missions which are, in nearly every case, larger than the parallel missions maintained by the small states. Thus, taking as a purely random sample the first thirty states covered by the (British) *Foreign Office List* for 1965, a comparison of the missions they maintain in London with the missions the United Kingdom maintains in their capitals yields the figures shown on next page for official members of the missions.[1]

It may be noted that, excluding the communist states which have their own special reasons for maintaining very large staffs with full diplomatic status, only Dahomey, Gabon and the Dominican Republic maintain larger staffs in Britain than Britain maintains in their capitals. London is generally considered a choice posting and the personal factor in this connexion cannot be overlooked. But for the rest, there is a fairly general discrepancy between the British staff abroad and the foreign staff in Britain which becomes even greater when British regular consular staff in provincial cities (not

---

[1] Including chief of mission, diplomatic officers, service and other specialist attachés, and career consuls working in the capital and therefore forming an integral and very useful part of the embassy wherever the head of the mission wishes them to.

TABLE I

	Embassy in London	UK Mission abroad
Afghanistan	3	7
Algeria	8	11
Argentine Republic	12	21
Austria	7	19
Belgium	14	22
Bolivia	3	9
Brazil	24	20
Bulgaria	8	7
Burma	12	26
Cameroon	6	8
Chile	7	17
China (C.P.R.)	17	13
Colombia	7	9
Congo (Leo.)	3	17
Costa Rica	4	5
Cuba	14	13
Czechoslovakia	24	11
Dahomey	5	4
Denmark	19	20
Dominican Republic	7	6
Ecuador	6	11
El Salvador	2	5
Ethiopia	4	13
Finland	11	19
France	43	43
Gabon	9	4
Germany, Fed. Rep. of	33	43
Greece	15	25
Guinea	4	7
Haiti	2	3

included in the table) are taken into account, as they perhaps should be. Thus the British staff in Burma is more than twice the Burmese in London. In Leopoldville it is almost six times as large, or even more if the four consular officials in provincial capitals are taken into consideration. Ethiopia, for which London remains an important foreign capital, maintains a very small embassy; the British Embassy in Addis Ababa is several times as large. In all these cases the discrepancies may be partly accounted for by the difference in the manner which various states conduct their business and the extent to which the central government is prepared to delegate negotiation to its distant representatives. Nevertheless, this alone cannot possibly account for the preponderance of British staff abroad either in these three capitals or, say, in Finland, where diplomatic and outlying consular staff together number twenty-six, while Finland maintains only eleven officers in a capital which is for it a most important political and commercial centre.

Secondly, the numerical discrepancy is usually as great when the total networks of diplomatic contacts available to small and great powers are compared. In 1961 France maintained ninety-nine Embassies and Legations exclusive of High Commissions in the French Community.[1] Britain, in 1965, maintained ninety-six diplomatic missions,[2] nineteen Commonwealth High Commissions and the Embassy in Ireland,[3] a total of 116 missions not counting delegations to the United Nations and other international and treaty organizations. Smaller states, even when they maintain formal diplomatic relations with a large number of other countries, generally restrict the number of missions they have abroad, some of which serve more than one country. Finland, in 1961, maintained full diplomatic relations with fifty-seven states, but missions in only thirty-three.[4] Here, of course, the importance which a small power ascribes to its relations with foreign states, and to which in particular, will be closely reflected. So will, in a more general manner, its own self-made picture of its role in international politics. Swedish representatives are accredited to no less than ninety-two states—many more than Finland's. But of these thirty

---

[1] Jean Baillou and Pierre Pelletier, *Les Affaires Étrangères*, Paris, 1962, p. 111.
[2] *Foreign Office List*, 1965.
[3] *Commonwealth Relations Office List*, 1965.
[4] *Facts About Finland*, Helsinki, 1961, pp. 61–62.

are non-resident and contacts with them cannot be anything but discontinuous, even infrequent. Furthermore, of the sixty-two missions in actual operation forty-four are composed of a head of mission and from one to three diplomatic or commercial officials. The remaining eighteen large missions maintained by Sweden show very clearly where that country's major business and interests lie: the great powers and Sweden's immediate neighbours, with few exceptions.[1]

Broadly speaking, therefore, and with due allowance for exceptional cases, the greater powers may be said to maintain nearly universal networks of diplomatic missions, each of which is fairly heavily staffed and backed by a proportionately large ministry at home, while the smaller states either restrict their diplomatic activities to those countries where their main interests lie—the greater powers and their immediate neighbours—or else maintain a fairly large network of small missions which can neither engage in more than quite limited political, commercial and consular work, nor are expected to.

Of the intelligence services, obviously much less can be said with any assurance. But it would seem reasonable—and, on the basis of the sparse information available from time to time, justifiable—to suppose that much the same were true. In other words, the great powers tend to try to back up their world-wide interests and activities with world-wide collection of information. The small powers, if they engage in intelligence operations at all, tend to limit them quite severely to targets of immediate concern.

The difference in scope between the diplomatic machines of small and great states is often accentuated by differences

---

[1] United States, USSR, United Kingdom, Japan, Federal Germany, France, Italy, India, Denmark, Finland, Norway, Netherlands, Poland, and Belgium, but also Canada, Argentina, Austria and Spain. Source: *Sveriges Statskalender*, 1964, pp. 306–17. Lest this be thought a peculiarity of industrial states, it may be noted that whereas Algeria maintains thirty-one missions of which over half are in Africa and the Middle East and a quarter in the major states, and Ethiopia maintains only twenty-four missions all but three of which are in these two categories, Egypt keeps up no less than seventy-nine full diplomatic missions. Source: *The Middle East and North Africa*, Europa Publications, 1965, pp. 108, 173–4 and 693–4.

of quality. It is generally the case that the professional competence and intellectual attainments of the diplomat representing a great power are higher than those of the small power's official. This is not universally true, by any means. The major posts—Washington, Paris, London and so forth—are usually headed and staffed by men of high quality irrespective of the country they represent. This would certainly be true of all those states which have had the time and leisure to build up an experienced diplomatic service. But at the minor posts—the majority—the differences are often clearly apparent. A small power finds it difficult to staff thirty, forty or even more missions with a full complement of trained, experienced and intellectually qualified men. Still less can it hope to maintain a complete foreign service, numbering perhaps two or three hundred or more, all of whose members are of the requisite quality. The major powers clearly find it less difficult, though their foreign services are many times larger.[1]

There would appear to be two reasons for this. One lies in the fact that it is easier to find several thousand adequately qualified men and women in a fully literate society of fifty or a hundred million than several hundred in an equally literate society of five or ten million, let alone a non-industrial one of anything between two and thirty million. But there is a second reason which is possibly more critical. Diplomatic work in the service of a great state, even one that is vestigially great, carries with it not insignificant compensations: the inherent interest of the work itself, a sense of personal contribution—however small—to great affairs, and no small measure of prestige while abroad. The service of a small power carries with it little prestige and, what is more important, is likely to be of real and sustained interest only

---

[1] The French Foreign Service is just under a thousand (Baillou and Pelletier, op. cit., p. 112—allowing for the posts in Africa not included in the figure published). The British Diplomatic Service numbers about 1,100 senior personnel. In 1954 the US Foreign Service numbered over 4,000, including both Department and Foreign Service staff *en poste* (Department of State, *Report of the Secretary of State's Committee of Personnel*, Washington, 1954, p. 61) and should now be substantially larger.

in those few great or neighbouring capitals where the state's really vital external affairs are handled. For the rest, as Sir William Hayter has put it (though in a slightly different context), 'oppressed with the futility of much diplomatic life, the fatiguing social round, the conferences that agree nothing, the dispatches that nobody reads, you begin to think that diplomacy is meaningless and that the world would be none the worse for its abolition.'[1] The foreign service officer of the small power, unless he is exceptionally fortunate, is caught between two mountains of indifference: his activities are of no more than marginal interest to the country in which he is serving and only of very little more interest to his own. This is not a situation likely to attract a nation's élite in large numbers.

The chief significance of these differences of scope and quality between the small and great powers' diplomatic machinery does not lie in the respective capacity for negotiation, still less in the sphere of representation—the least demanding of the diplomatic functions. It lies in the sphere of information and intelligence, in knowledge of affairs, in the availability of data on matters as they arise and, if possible, before they arise, which is to say, in the capacity to prepare one's moves and execute them with the least risk of failure and with the highest probability of having chosen the correct alternative. This is, certainly, a question of potential and not necessarily actual, competence, efficiency and success: the diplomatic history of great powers is replete with examples of misused, ignored or misleading intelligence and specialist advice. But there is nevertheless a marked difference between having information available should one choose to examine it and act upon it and not having it at all.

What emerges from a comparison of the great and small powers' diplomatic machinery is, in fact, a vast disparity in the information available and in the quality and size of the machinery designed to deal with it at specialist level. In plain terms this has three consequences. Firstly, a small

[1] Hayter, op. cit., pp. 73–74.

power's expertise is limited to its own geographical sur-
roundings, but is not, for that reason, necessarily superior to
the great power's expertise on the identical region. For the
rest, its information is either superficial or non-existent.
Secondly, the great power's net, being cast world-wide,
ought, in principle, to enhance that power's tactical advantage, operational competence and sheer prestige in all great
international affairs. It usually does. Thirdly, the great
power is almost always in a position of superiority over the
small state with regard to their respective abilities to know of
and evaluate *each other's* moves. Once again, this is a potential, not necessarily actual ability; as a rule, there are rather
more exceptions to it than in the case of the first two points
made.

The disparity of information available to the official
external relations machinery is deepened by disparities in
the field of secret intelligence. Communist bloc states apart,
small countries do not readily engage in intelligence operations directed against great powers, while the reverse is
obviously not true. There is a sense in which all states are
intelligence targets for great powers. This assymetry is
partly the result of the expense, political risks and operational
problems peculiar to secret intelligence. It is, for example,
inherently unlikely that a defector from the service of a great
power should transfer his allegiance to a small, unaligned
state. The ideological background to such a move would
seem unimaginably complex and considerations of personal
safety would generally militate against it. But the more important and fundamental reason for the common inhibition
of small powers in this respect, as opposed to the almost total
lack of inhibition of great powers, lies in profound differences of outlook as to what constitutes the most effective,
and at the same time the permissible, pattern of international
behaviour. This will be referred to in some detail later in this
chapter.

There is one last point to make in this connexion. Unlike
normal diplomatic activity, modern intelligence operations

may have a very large and costly technological element. Aerial photography by high altitude aircraft is an obvious, but nonetheless characteristic example. Here the problems of research and development and spiralling cost are very similar to those in the field of weapons design and production. This technological element goes some of the way to explain the vast sums that appear to be devoted to intelligence by the United States Government.[1] The expense of such operations automatically restricts the small power both quantitatively and qualitatively.

Rough equality of diplomatic and intelligence apparatus in the regional sphere (at best), distinct inequality beyond the immediate geographical neighbourhood and very probable inequality in their relations with each other—these, then, are the common and largely unavoidable disparities in the machinery available to the small and to the great power respectively. They may be very much greater;[2] they are unlikely to be less. Great effort and investment, a high degree of devotion and patriotic endeavour and sheer flair may narrow the gap somewhat. They can hardly do more. The small state which is in close alliance with a great power will probably have the benefits of its protection and assistance in these as in other fields. The unaligned state will not, or only fleetingly and with respect to some concrete tactical situation. For the fields of diplomacy and intelligence are naturally those which, in the nature of things, are most sensitive to political calculation.

What this fundamental state of inequality means in practice, that is in the elaboration and definition of foreign policy is, however, a quite separate question. A large, efficient and knowledgeable diplomatic and intelligence machine may enhance the self-confidence of the policy-

---

[1] The figure may be as large as an annual $4,000 million, of which half is spent by the CIA and half by other intelligence agencies. Cf. David Wise and Thomas B. Ross, *The Invisible Government*, 1965, pp. 259–60.

[2] In the Italo-Abyssinian war, an extreme and limiting case, the superiority of Italian Intelligence was precisely parallel to their technical superiority in other fields. Cf. Leonard Mosley, *Haile Selassie*, 1964, p. 218.

maker and it may imbue him with a sense of well being and with an illusion of power that is exhilarating. The smooth control of any piece of intricate machinery, even a bureaucratic one, tends to be very satisfying. If, as Harold Lasswell has expressed it, 'the political type is characterized by an intense and ungratified craving for deference,'[1] there is perhaps no equal to a foreign ministry or even a large embassy for providing it. This is a point of some importance, as will be shown below. But how well the machine is actually used and, particularly, to what extent and in what manner its collective knowledge and experience constitute real components of the policy adopted and of the decisions taken must clearly depend, however, on another set of factors. First among these would appear to be what might be called the administrative distance or gap between the level of activity where the store of isolated data and expertise relevant to the particular issue is to be found and the level at which the policy-makers themselves actually operate. This distance is not a simple function of the purely hierarchal gap between government, minister and perhaps senior officials on the one hand and, say, the embassy and regional division on the other. It depends first and foremost on the nature and size of the government machine as a whole and on the range of topics which are of immediate concern to the government in its external relations. It therefore depends, ultimately, on the size and power of the state in question.

For the great state with real or supposed world-wide interests the processes of policy-making are extremely complex. This is particularly the case in the open societies where a high level of public discussion of foreign policy issues obtains. But in closed societies too it must be supposed that if the machinery available is allowed and encouraged to perform its professional function the formulation of policy cannot be simple. In the great power the bureaucracy is vast and its procedures necessarily intricate. The problem of adjusting, integrating and resolving the dis-

[1] Harold Dwight Lasswell, *Power and Personality*, New York, 1948, p. 38.

parate and often conflicting information, views and proposals of the various administrative bodies and pressure groups concerned with foreign affairs is a very difficult one. The multiple interests of the state bring it into contact, and therefore potential conflict or disagreement, with most other sovereign nations. The number of questions that may arise in a given period of time and without necessarily being related to each other may be very great. And the volume of information and official advice flowing into the machine and up through its hierarchy is far beyond the capacity of the inevitably small group of policy-makers to absorb unless it is carefully but drastically whittled down to manageable proportions.

The Quai d'Orsay, administering a service which is by no means prone to transmit and circulate information for its own sake, handles close to two million words of enciphered telegrams a month,[1] or probably enough to fill a printed book of some 150 pages each day. Approximately 80,000 telegrams arrived in Paris from missions abroad in the course of 1959,[2] or about 200 a day. And this, it must be remembered is only the tip of a mountain, the bulk of which is made up of vast quantities of dispatches and purely overt material culled by missions all over the world. The British figures are very similar.[3] Put in another way the Foreign Office spends £2 million a year, or about 7 per cent. of its total budget, on communications alone.[4] What the Soviet telegraphic and courier traffic amounts to cannot be estimated, but with their tradition of near-total coverage and multiplicity of overlapping agencies[5] it must be many times as great.

But, since information welling up through the official channels has never been thought sufficient in iteslf, press and

---

[1] Baillou and Pelletier, op. cit., p. 124.   [2] Ibid., p. 159.
[3] *Report of the Committee on Representational Services Overseas*, 1964, Cmnd. 2276, p. 7.
[4] Ibid., p. 159.
[5] Including the Foreign Ministry proper, the KGB, the GRU, TASS, and the presumably less systematic channels of Party inter-communication.

parliament—where they exist and are free—may be very powerful centres of information and opinion. This is particularly so in the United States where the two are closely interrelated and the press, both indirectly through Congress and directly through its contacts with the State Department and the other agencies of the Administration, plays a considerable role as an informant. Of still greater importance is the manner in which the American press may give certain issues greater prominence than they might otherwise have and raise them higher on the Administration's list of priorities.[1]

The heart of the problem is the difficulty—perhaps impossibility—of creating order out of the cross-currents of conflicting forces that face the great power abroad and out of the welter of highly detailed, yet unavoidably uneven and imperfectly related information that accumulates at home.[2] Its counter-part is an unending search for coherence. To some extent this is a psychological need, generally felt very strongly in the United States, less so in Europe, and more obviously powerful in its effect in ideologically oriented states than in free societies. But equally it is an operational necessity and the greater the span and range of the power's concern and interests, the greater the difficulty of formulating, let alone executing, a coherent policy. In practical terms this means the need to talk in as few voices as possible, to give clear instructions to one's representatives which, while being properly applicable in substance in each case, do not conflict with each other, and, lastly, to be able to link the policy pursued with respect to one issue or nation to that pursued with respect to another. This is often extremely difficult even when the pattern of relationships is, so to speak, only triangular. American policy towards Indonesia could *not* be squared in a satisfactory way with its policy

---

[1] See Bernard G. Cohen, 'Foreign Policy Makers and the Press', in James N. Rosenau (Ed.), *International Politics and Foreign Policy*, New York, 1961, pp. 223–5.
[2] Cf. Theodore C. Sorensen, *Decision-Making in the White House*, New York, 1963, especially pp. 36–42.

towards the Netherlands in one period and Malaysia in another. The geometry may be more complex—as in the Middle East and in Latin America—and the overlapping and conflicting interests and pressures of foreign states and domestic opinion defy attempts to reduce them to a manageable and sufficiently comprehensive analytical pattern out of which the correct and coherent approach will duly emerge. Either way, if the result is not to be a temporary abstention from the taking of any decision, the solution must lie in choice, in a form of surgery. And this, in turn, requires a principle or rule or previous formulation by which matters may be judged, compared and decided. How was the United States to determine its position with respect to the Dutch–Indonesian conflict over West Irian when it came to a head in 1961 and further postponement of a decision appeared even less desirable than the probable consequences of whatever decision was adopted? Clearly, this could only be done by considering the conflict in a wider, or at any rate different context where formulations of policy on other matters, closer to the direct interests of the United States, could be brought to bear and a new pattern of analysis, neither Indonesian nor Dutch, could be applied. In this case, the operative considerations were, of course, the Cold War in two concrete respects: firstly, to avoid encouraging Indonesia to align itself permanently with the opposition; secondly, to avoid 'a great-power confrontation in the Banda Sea with Moscow and Peking backing Indonesia while America backed the Dutch; like Laos, West New Guinea did not seem [to Kennedy] a part of the world in which great powers should be rationally engaged.'[1] The American analysis may well be thought erroneous in this particular case, but in terms of *method* this process of referring back in order to make clear political and intellectual sense of an otherwise tediously complex subject, is classic.

The aspects of great power policy-making discussed here

[1] Schlesinger, op. cit., p. 464.

are important to the small power in several ways. Firstly, it follows that at the higher levels of the great power policy-making machinery acquaintance with the affairs of the small power must necessarily be limited and intermittent. Secondly, the quest for coherence of policy impels the makers of it to consider the problems of the small state and their own relations with it—however amicably they may be disposed towards it on other grounds—in the light of considerations which are not directly relevant to the small state itself and which it can only influence marginally. There may follow a *dialogue de sourds* in which minds cannot meet, not necessarily because of ill-will, but because the attention of each side is fastened on matters and interests which are largely or entirely unrelated. Lastly, the compulsion (already referred to) to view affairs in a very broad perspective where generalities count for very much more than details tends to encourage an approach that seizes upon the common characteristic of all small states—their absolute weakness—and ignores the highly differentiated circumstances in which each is placed.[1] This has certain consequences which will be considered in the third section of this chapter.

The making of small power foreign policy is conducted on a different scale, in a different manner and out of somewhat different materials. The range of political problems judged real and relevant is much reduced. The machinery maintained for the collection and interpretation of information is, as has been noted, generally smaller in size, probably less efficacious, and focused on a limited number of subjects. Where the great affairs of the world impinge on them directly, the leaders of a small power will therefore generally find themselves operating in the light of their own regional interests, conflicts and fears. Only on such subjects can there normally be the necessary combination of assembled infor-

---

[1] One of the important considerations that helped President Kennedy make his mind up about West Irian was that 'the President regarded Indonesia, this country of a hundred million people, so rich in oil, tin and rubber, as one of the potentially significant nations of Asia.' (Schlesinger, op. cit., p. 464). The Netherlands, by implication, was not in the same class.

mation and fully thought-out lines of conduct. Where detailed knowledge of extra-regional matters is possessed it is of necessity borrowed, which is to say, that it comes from non-autonomous sources. This does not mean that it is inaccurate or unhelpful, but only that the processes of compilation and interpretation of world events and international forces in the clear light of one's own national interests that play so great a role in the policy-making of great powers does not take place at all. The result is that when a small power's leader thinks of affairs with which he and his officials are not directly concerned he is hard put not to be powerfully influenced by the views emanating from the great capitals. Alternatively, his thinking will contain an important intuitive element. The result may be shrewder and the state may be none the worse off. But the fact that the leader and his officials cannot compete in systematic analysis of world affairs with their opposite numbers in the great states may put them at a psychological and dialectical disadvantage in certain circumstances—as when, in the course of the dialogue with the great power, the terms are shifted to what is for the small state the more abstract level of considerations of international significance. For the more perceptive leaders of small powers this may lead to a more or less conscious opting out from close examination of certain subjects, even to an acceptance of a kind of political provinciality. Thus Prince Sihanouk, explaining his policy towards China in the deliberately simple terms of fear of Thailand and Vietnam:

La Chine, j'en ai besoin. Que j'aime ce grand peuple ou non, je tiens que sans la contre-assurance qu'il m'offre contre mes voisins, je risquerais fort de succomber.[1]

With a smaller machinery at hand and with a narrower range of problems and topics to deal with, coherence of policy is fairly easily attained. For the small state which is outside the protection of a great power this coherence is enhanced by the precariousness and the dangers implicit in its exposed position and which concentrate its collective mind

---

[1] *Le Monde*, 24 June 1964, reprinted in *Survival*, September–October 1964.

wonderfully. Furthermore, within the limits set by the nature of the problem and the extent of their other pre-occupations, the policy-makers can themselves become personally familiar with the detail of the topics they are most concerned with. The influence of the bureaucracy is therefore much reduced and decisions are more apt to be taken without or despite its advice and with far less inhibition than might be the case in great powers. When the Russians in April, 1938, initiated the negotiations that were later to lead to the Winter War, the Finnish Prime and Foreign Ministers thought nothing of handling them for a long time by themselves. Not even all the Cabinet was informed. This was no doubt due partly to the Russian demand for secrecy, but it was certainly reciprocated by the Finnish leaders. The professional advice of their chief military counsellor, Mannerheim, was rejected even though he was, over and above his purely military capacity, the man who knew and understood Russia in general and the Russian pre-occupation with the defence of Leningrad in particular better than any one of them.[1] In the small state *all* those concerned with major policy are, in a sense, specialists—or see themselves as such. In such circumstances the professional apparatus is unlikely to attain the kind of prestige and influence it sometimes possesses in great states.

The fact that there may thus be a more personal, less institutional influence on the making of policy tends to sharpen its definition, producing a more direct, less generalized formulation and conception of affairs. There is a greater likelihood that it be the product of a single, dominant mind and less that of a committee striving for a comprehensive view. Perception of affairs is more direct, less influenced by, and less dependent on, advisers. There may be a great and

---

[1] Cf. Väinö Tanner, *The Winter War*, Stanford, 1957, p. 3 et. seq., and Marshal Mannerheim, *Memoirs*, 1953, p. 293 et. seq. Also comments on Mannerheim and his relations with the Finnish political leaders in Anthony F. Upton, *Finland in Crisis, 1940–1941*, 1964, pp. 37–38. It is not clear whether the Finnish Foreign Ministry was ever asked for its professional advice, but it seems not to have been nor even to have played an operative role of any importance.

significant element of personal insight; and by the same token there may more easily develop an element of passion and personal involvement that is certainly not unknown in great states, but is nonetheless infrequently found, or substantially muted and absorbed by the machine in practice. In the great powers the impassioned handling of external affairs —as with Eden over Suez—is commonly viewed as something of an aberration. In the small power it is not. It is rather the cool, collective wisdom apparent in Swedish foreign policy over the past three decades that seems unusual, even a little odd.

Personal conviction, intuitive interpretation of affairs and a political environment which compels the statesman to distinguish quite sharply between what is relevant to him and what is not—these are not disadvantages in themselves. But they do mean that quite a lot of the political-philosophical baggage that the small power statesman will have developed over the years is likely to enter into the elaboration of policy and certainly into his reactions—considered or intuitive—to external events and pressures. Along with the general political and ideological positions, the prejudice, the *idées fixes* and the other habits of thought that are found in any adult and certainly in the 'political type' (Lasswell's phrase), there cannot but be a strong, though not necessarily fully-formulated, view of the limits of his country's strength. This is a subject which no one with public responsibility in a small country can have failed to dwell upon at length, if only in the recesses of his mind.

Thus statesmen of both the small state and, as we have seen, the great state too, are liable to approach relations with each other in a frame of mind of which a general view of the small power as a species to which certain attitudes and considerations are appropriate, while others are not, is an important component. It is in the light of these considerations that, consciously or otherwise, the specific and concrete elements of the issue before them tend to be judged.

III

Weakness is the most common, natural and pervasive view of self in the small state and it afflicts its leaders and influences their behaviour in many ways, fathering a host of ready-made judgments on what is and what is not possible in various circumstances. It is the dominant fact of the state's international existence. It is unpleasant to be aware of it, either in strategic or human terms, and it often leads to a search for compensation or for an attitude which, when struck, reduces its significance. It is also easy to lapse into a form of moral surrender, into a somewhat pathetic posture:

Les petits États ne pourront jamais, ni au point de vue militaire ni au point de vue économique, rivaliser avec des colosses comme les États-Unis, l'Empire britannique ou l'U.R.S.S. Ils n'aspirent même pas a cette égalité: c'est dans d'autres domaines qu'ils placent leur ambition et leur fierté. Tout ce qu'ils demandent, c'est leur droit de vivre une vie nationale indépendente, de développer leur prospérité matérielle et de garder intacts leur patrimoine spirituelle. C'est pour ces valeurs-la qu'ils désirent vivre et c'est pour les sauvegarder que leurs citoyens sont prêts a prendre les armes.

Contre l'inégalité de fait entre petits États et grandes puissances, on peut se revolter, mais mieux vaut s'y résigner et en tirer le meilleur parti possible. L'histoire, cette grande consolatrice, est là, encore une fois, pour nous montrer qui sur le plan international, la puissance politique, militaire et économique est éphémère. 'Hier une grande Puissance, aujourd'hui un pauvre État' pourrait-on dire.[1]

Other writers have struck more pugnacious notes: 'The population of the country amounts to no more than a two-thousandth part of the human race, [but] the foundation of Swiss relf-respect is not to be imperilled by reference to these unpretentious figures.'[2] But the same sense of irremediable distress is there; and it is not unnatural that the distasteful, sometimes humiliating hierarchy of power be replaced by a more satisfying, moral one where the great

---

[1] Laszlo Ledermann, *Considérations sur le Petit État*, Neuchâtel, 1946, pp. 62–63.
[2] Fritz Ernst, *European Switzerland*, Zürich, 1951, p. 5.

powers, with their egoism and brutality, their collective role as prime mover in the international system, are suitably compared with the weaker class of states who being weaker are supposed, by that very fact, to be more likely to have justice on their side.[1]

Moral superiority and philosophical views lose much of their value, however, when the distance between the observer and the impact of great power pressure is reduced. They cannot compensate for frustration, fear and the general sense of helplessness, or for irritation at being excluded from the inner councils of one's own allies and having to listen to voices that consistently ignore the right and title of a small power to some say in world affairs.[2] After the trauma of violated pledges, shattered neutrality and barbarous invasion, the small states of Western Europe sought or accepted a political solution which seemed to offer some small hope of retaining a measure of influence over their national destinies.

Si les pays de Benelux lient leur sort à celui des Grandes Puissances, il nous semble justifié d'insister à ce qu'ils puissent faire entendre leur voix quand il s'agira de prendre des décisions qui pourront constituer une menace de la paix mondiale.

Thus the Dutch Foreign Minister at the signing of the Brussels Treaty in March 1948, ending a century of neutrality.[3]

Finally, there is stubbornness and dignity to fall back on— as for the Finns in 1940 and again at the conclusion of the world war—or a somewhat sentimental and puritanical

---

[1] 'There was a tendency in Sweden [between the two world wars] to range other States in a sort of order of rank. After Sweden there came (1) the Scandinavian countries, (2) the ex-Neutral small States, (3) the small States in general. On this point positive values were reversed: the Great Powers were regarded in the Swedish debate [on foreign policy] almost exclusively as the villains of the piece.' Herbert Tingsten, *The Debate on the Foreign Policy of Sweden*, 1949, p. 303.

[2] Cf. C. J. Hambro, *How to Win the Peace*, 1943, p. 92. Among the writers on the new world order he particularly complained about were Lord (David) Davies, Julian Huxley and Quincy Wright. Hambro was the last President of the League of Nations.

[3] Text in S. I. P. van Campen, *The Quest for Security*, The Hague, 1958, p. 65.

withdrawal from a hostile world which must be kept at bay—
as in South Africa today.[1]

Consciousness of one's own weakness and surrender to it,
or a sense of indignation or of moral superiority, or the felt
need to justify oneself, to apologize, or to prove one's worth
(to whom and in what court?),[2] or the retreat into inflexibility, or the adoption of a pathetic or heroic stance—all
these are personal, or at most social responses. It may be
questioned whether they really have much to do with the
making of a state's foreign policy, whatever the state. But, as
we have tried to show, the assessment of situations in the
face of incomplete knowledge and a surplus of data, is
governed in small states to a very considerable degree by the
outlook of the personalities involved in the making of
policy—much more so than in great states. Furthermore,
these responses are only partly irrational or emotional in
content. In part they are—or are derived from—intellectual
and ideological positions. Consequently, they are extremely
important in the public formulation and justification of
foreign policy. The extent to which the public view is, or
may be made to be, coincident with the government's is, of
course, vital to the ability of the latter to carry the public
with them. The long pull and the great intensity of effort
which, as will be shown, are the pre-conditions for the success of any small state in its attempt to maintain a significant
degree of economic, military and political independence,
require such public support. And the support, where given,
will be in such generalized, somewhat emotional forms.
What these responses to the perception of weakness have in
common is a high degree of self-consciousness and a strong
sense that a small state is inherently and structurally a weak
political entity, shot through with disabilities and short-

---

[1] See J. E. Spence, *Republic under Pressure*, 1965, Chapter 2. The picture may
be compared with J. C. Smuts' book *A Century of Wrong*, published at the outbreak
of the Boer War.

[2] Cf. Hubert Ripka, 'Small and Great Nations', *Czechoslovak Documents and
Sources*, No. 9, 1944. The pamphlet is an apologia for small states and a denial of
all that is implied by the twin terms Balkanization and *Kleinstaaterei*.

comings. By way of both psychological and material compensation it has only mental values and capabilities to draw on: determination, canniness, unity and patience. It follows that where these are lacking or are eroded by pressure, failure and defeat, it becomes extremely difficult to keep the ship on its course and under control. It may be thought impossible to keep it afloat; the attempt will then be abandoned.

The assymetry that pervades the relations between great and small states and the lack of military, political and economic balance affect the thinking of great power statesmen no less than small. More than anything else it tends to simplify their outlook. For the great power, the small state is either irrelevant to its purpose, a marginal factor of support, or an impediment (but not a barrier) to the pursuit of its interests. It may be an opponent, but not a rival. Its inner workings, as has been noted, are unlikely to be well known or understood to the great power policy-makers, perhaps not even to the specialists. When it comes into their vision it tends to be in the context of a more general, more important issue. As a result it is hard indeed not to deal with it, conceptually, as an object, something less than fully organic, in fact a member of a different species. What this may mean in practice—contempt, disdain, disinterest, coldness, inflexibility or simple impatience—depends on the nature of the issue at stake and the importance attached to it. It also depends on the nature of the great power's society and régime. But so far as a generic characteristic is in question, it is this unwillingness or, in some cases, inability to ascribe to the small state quite the same value and rights that a great nation's leaders ascribe in the most natural way to themselves. Where other great powers are concerned the effects of this common attitude to an alien society are mitigated by the need to accommodate one's purposes to theirs. Where the small power is in view no such mitigation need occur. So Zhdanov may complacently regret that the Soviet Union did not occupy Finland at the end of the war and Molotov may entirely dismiss Finland as 'a peanut'.[1] And on the other hand and at another extreme of good-humoured disdain, Roosevelt may dismiss Siam's declaration of war against the United States in 1942 as unworthy of any reaction at all, and only condescend to inform the House and Senate foreign affairs committees, quite informally, that such a declaration had been issued.[2] Power generates self-confidence and egotism very easily. Very great power seems to engender a certain self-righteousness as well. Psychologically, its function seems to be to provide a moral basis for the political exploitation of preponderant strength and is thus interesting to compare with the not altogether dissimilar manner in which the leaders and ideologues of small nations compensate for their perceived weakness. So far as the great powers are concerned nowhere is this moral complacency so apparent today as in the campaign waged against the proliferation of nuclear weapons. And, indeed, in the context of this great question the relations between the great and small powers as classes of states with distinct and characteristic views of the way in which the world may or ought to be ordered are laid quite bare.[3] 'In politics and strategy, as in economics, monopoly naturally appears to him who enjoys it as the best system.'[4]

IV

Not all states attempt to examine their international position and formulate their policy in a truly systematic way. Among those which do make the attempt, the small states, as we have seen, are in fact precluded from succeeding in more than a limited degree and with respect to more than a narrow range of topics. But nowhere can the process ever be fully systematic, fully scientific. The uncertainty and confusion that are characteristic of international affairs until a pattern has been invented for them by the analyst—be he official or unofficial, systematic in his method or intuitive—

[1] Milovan Djilas, *Conversations with Stalin*, 1962, p. 140.
[2] Elliott Roosevelt (Ed.), *The Roosevelt Letters*, 1952, iii., p. 414.
[3] See Chapter 9 below.
[4] General de Gaulle, press conference, 14 January 1963.

leave much room for the influence of general ideas and of particular ways of observing events and determining their relevance to one's own interests. It follows that the great disparity of resources and of machinery between small and great states and the cumulative effect of historic experience on either side, cannot but influence the thinking of their leaders with respect to each other. And the disparate thinking cannot but govern to a significant degree the decisions taken and the lines of conduct adopted.

For the small power which has not abandoned the attempt to pursue a course laid out with clear and primary reference to its own national interests this means two things. Firstly, it must cope with the fact that in its relations with the great power the preponderance of physical strength in the latter will be buttressed by inequality in the instruments of foreign policy and by a combination of indifference and deep-rooted reluctance to ascribe any practical significance to the doctrine of the legal equality of states.

Secondly, this means that in the processes of its own decision-making and in the execution of its own foreign policy, the small power is forever liable to deflection and disturbance through reconsideration of fundamental questions about its own situation, role, purposes and capabilities.

The result is an element of permanent inhibition and doubt as to what is the wisest course to adopt. Only very exceptional men with great intuitive gifts and a marked capacity and readiness for the taking of risks and for facing powerful opposition are likely to overcome these disabilities and imbue their colleagues and their public with their own self-confidence.

3

ECONOMIC DISABILITIES[1]

I

No country can hope to supply all its needs from within its own territory. The smaller it is the higher the probability that the range of its domestic resources will be a narrow one. The higher its level of economic and social development (and corresponding per capita income) the greater will be the range of its needs. Its needs are also likely to vary to some extent with the intensity of the political difficulties it experiences in its foreign relations: these can easily lead to the drawing up of great lists of military requirements which can be met only partly by local industry, perhaps not at all.[2] But a wide range of requirements—civil or military—necessarily implies either foreign assistance on a very great scale or extensive foreign trade. For the isolated or unaligned state the former is rarely feasible, politically; and if it is, is at best a short-term arrangement which cannot be relied on for long. Extensive foreign trade is therefore the *sine qua non* of economic and social progress as well as of any substantial effort to give political independence a material (i.e. military and diplomatic) foundation. Imports are needed to satisfy consumer requirements, exports must be marketed to pay for these imports and also for the equipment, fuel and raw materials needed by the export industries themselves. The narrower the range of domestic resources the greater will be the need to import what is lacking. This applies to human,

[1] The purpose of this chapter is to isolate a number of economic factors which are characteristic of small states and which bear directly on their *political* relations with other, greater powers. A full-dress, technical discussion of the general economic problems posed by limited size is to be found in E. A. G. Robinson (Ed.), *Economic Consequences of the Size of Nations*, London, 1960, passim.

[2] The problem of defence requirements is discussed in Chapter 4 below.

no less than material resources—witness the great influx
of migrant labour into industrial Europe in recent
years.

Broadly speaking, much of this is true in one degree or
another of all states. But the smaller the state the more
rapidly these requirements multiply and the more acutely
they are felt. Perhaps only the greatest of all can, at least in
principle, attain total self-sufficiency. In practice, even
Russia and the United States tend increasingly to extend
their foreign trading. But at the other end of the spectrum of
size and development only the entirely undeveloped and
non-developing states can—in principle, again—opt out of
foreign trade and then only if they are prepared to bear the
social and political consequences of such stagnation. In
practice none do. The political, social and military penalties
for forgoing economic and technological advance are rightly
(and almost universally) believed to be heavier than the
difficulties of coping with the problem of development. It is,
of course, also true that in many important respects the
problems that face the small developing state are *initially*
very much akin, if not identical, to those that face the large
developing countries. But the somewhat paradoxical and
certainly disheartening effect of development in the small
state is that the higher it rises in the ladders of consumption
and technology the more rapidly the difficulties multiply
and the greater are the obstacles to each successive step
than is the case, *ceteris paribus*, in large developing countries.

Not all these difficulties are capable of precise correlation
with the size of states—by whatever standard that may be
measured. Every case is in some respects unique. Clearly a
state like Switzerland, almost bare of natural resources for
industry and with very limited areas of arable land is less
fortunate than Sweden which is at least extraordinarily
wealthy in timber and metals. But there remains the inherent
probability that a small state will have resources which are
severely limited in *kind*, if not in quantity and it may there-

fore be assumed that even in the most fortunate cases much will be lacking.

In some respects difficulties of this kind are also found where a large, highly developed state is, relative to its size, exceptionally poor in arable land or local sources of energy and raw materials for manufacture. Japan is an obvious example. But while Japan conforms to the pattern common to small states of its level of development in this respect of marked inability to satisfy needs from local resources and of a very high degree of foreign trading,[1] its size spares it from what is possibly a still more crucial characteristic disability of small powers. The nub of the matter is that the small national economy provides a small domestic market and a small market generally implies limited domestic demand for particular goods and services. This in turn would normally mean small firms and a high incidence of diseconomies of scale in production. But since the small state must export extensively to provide its consumers with a full range of requirements and do so in a proportionately much higher degree than the large state its firms cannot avoid competition in the international market with those of the great states whose *absolute* stake in world trade is of course very great indeed. And here the dice are loaded against it.

In principle there is probably nothing that can be produced within a small national economy that cannot be produced in a large one. But the reverse of this proposition would certainly be untrue. The greater the domestic market, the greater and more varied the supply of raw materials, the greater the probability of there being local resources of cheap energy, and the greater the relative mobility and variety of manpower, clearly the greater will be the probability that a given good can be produced and marketed cheaply and efficiently. After-sale services and marketing organizations can be more extensive. Frequently the quality of the product will be higher. These are the inherent advantages of a large economy

---

[1] This can be seen clearly in Table IV, with due allowance for the effect of Japan's geographical remoteness from its chief trading partners.

and they stem from the sheer scale of production and of market that are possible.[1]

Firms in the small economy, if they are to be fully competitive with those of the larger, must operate on a similar scale, i.e. be of a comparable order of physical and financial magnitude. From the point of view of the national economy as a whole this would mean that in respect of certain products it would be behaving in its *external* trading like a major one. But in practice this means, firstly, that it must specialize, rather than diversify its business; and secondly, that the few and favoured large industries would lack the underpinning of a large domestic market. This makes for special sensitivity to market fluctuations both in respect of the product itself and in respect of those imported materials or energy supplies needed for its manufacture.

Broadly speaking these factors affect all small states—and some larger developing states too, at any rate in the initial stages of their advance towards industrialization. But certain distinctions between those states whose exports are predominantly industrial goods and those which are principally exporters of primary products may be made.

A very useful attempt to express the degree of specialization in a limited number of export commodities with some precision has been made by M. Michaely[2] who has examined the export patterns of thirty-two nations trading in 150 commodities and abstracted the following 'coefficients of commodity concentration' (such that the highest possible coefficient is 100, where all exports are of a single good, and the lowest coefficient is about eight, where the country's exports are equally divided among the 150 commodities).

Firstly, the figures illustrate very clearly the difference in export patterns between industrial and non-industrial

---

[1] Needless to say there will always be a host of minor exceptions to this pattern where special skills or a highly particularized product provide a near-monopoly (e.g. diamond cutting or Scotch whisky), or where demand is so great that the cost factor temporarily ceases to be decisive.

[2] Michael Michaely, *Concentration in International Trade*, Amsterdam, 1962, p. 16. (Dr. Michaely's criteria of 'size' differ slightly, but not significantly, from those used throughout this study.)

TABLE II

	Developed countries	Under-developed countries	Total
Large countries	21·1	57·9	40·6
Small countries	39·1	52·0	43·4
Total	31·1	55·8	41·9

states. Secondly, they illustrate still more strikingly the difference between the export patterns of large industrial states and small industrial states, the coefficient of commodity concentration in the latter being almost twice that of the former. Thirdly, they would seem to support the thesis that while the difference between large and small non-industrial states is not very significant (in the present context), the *transition* to an industrial economy is not likely to release the small under-developed state from the penalties of specialization to the same extent that it is likely to release the large one.

Some small industrial states have been very successful in their efforts to behave in their foreign trading in much the same manner as greater states. The Netherlands provide a notable example with at least four enterprises of very large size, comparable in every way with the greatest of their kind elsewhere. Two (the Shell group and Unilever) are, significantly enough, part British. The other two (Philips and Aku) are predominantly Dutch, however. Philips had a turn-over of £650 million in 1964. It maintains sixty-three plants in the Netherlands (and more plants in thirty countries overseas); it is in the running for a place as the world's third largest electronics concern; it has marketing subsidiaries in fifty-six countries; and it accounts for an eighth of all Holland's industrial exports. Aku is smaller; but its sales in 1964 still accounted for some £250 million, and it exports *two-thirds* of all that it produces in Holland.[1]

But there are obvious limits to this process: a high level of

[1] *Economist*, 6 March 1965, pp. 1009–13.

development means ever greater diversity of requirements, while the higher the degree of specialization the greater will be the consequent dependence on foreign markets and foreign suppliers. Even if the risks involved in such dependence were judged acceptable, there would remain a very wide range of domestic requirements for goods and services (certain foods, medical care, education, administration, &c.) which can neither be imported nor exported usefully. This, incidentally, helps to explain why the condition of underdevelopment—regardless of the size of the state—allows a higher degree of specialization in trade than that of development.

In practice, the risks of very extensive foreign trade are great. The small industrial power is generally dependent to a much higher extent than the larger industrial power (with the notable exceptions of the United Kingdom and Japan) on imported goods and materials both for domestic consumption and for processing and re-export. Fluctuations in the supply and price of imports may radically affect the general price level in the country, and, by extension, the cost calculations of the export industry, in a much broader manner than simply through the direct effect on industrial costs of price changes in raw materials. The smaller the nation and the more highly concentrated its economic activities in chosen fields, the greater will be the damage to the economy as a whole as a result of isolated change abroad.

The small, industrial power suffers other characteristic disadvantages. Its limited aggregate resources make it extremely difficult for it to engage in the kind of massive scientific and technological research and development programmes which are essential to modern industry and which the greater powers with which it is in competition can permit themselves. France, with great agricultural as well as industrial strength, plans to devote no less than 2·5 per cent. of its Gross National Product to research and development by 1970. No small power, however wealthy, is in a position to siphon off so large a fraction of its total resources. And it is of course the *absolute* magnitude of resources that is really decisive in research and development.

Again, while the market for manufactured goods as a whole is generally more stable than that for primary products, the market for a *specific* manufactured good is not necessarily so. The factors governing it are more numerous and intricate and the effects of technological change and the periodic shifts in taste and consumer requirements can be very great, even decisive. Yet the small power must attempt a far higher degree of concentration of its capacity in specific industries, putting relatively more eggs in single baskets than the greater powers need do, and with objective limits on even this process, as has been suggested. The small exporting nation is in permanent competition with the great industrial states and the competition is unequal.

Finally, while the small power must, ideally, strive to gain the advantages of economy of scale by specializing on the production (exporting) side, it will of course remain relatively unspecialized on the consumption side. And although (except for the comparatively rare cases of giant enterprises like Philips) it will have to rely on a limited number of relatively large markets for its products, it will itself, as a consumer, constitute a multitude of small markets. Its power to exploit the latter in favour of the former will be correspondingly weak.

Partly for geographical, partly for historical reasons, and partly because it would generally be pointless and inefficient for a small exporting nation to attempt, of its own volition, to operate in a great number of foreign markets when its total productive capacity may often be easily absorbed by a single foreign market, small states tend to concentrate their exports geographically, as well as qualitatively. This is true both of states which export primary products and those whose exports are predominantly industrial goods.

Michaely has shown this very clearly by examining a group of forty-four trading nations and calculating 'coefficients of geographic concentration of exports', as follows[1]:

TABLE III

	Developed countries	Under-developed countries	Total
Large countries	29·1	45·7	37·4
Small countries	37·9	58·7	44·9
Total	34·0	50·7	41·0

What this means, in effect, is that the small state's pattern of trade is more restricted than that of the large state. The number of suppliers and customers is more limited. In the case of very many under-developed states the pattern of trade may be founded on one overwhelming supplier or customer; and supplier and customer are often identical. To some extent this is because commodity trading—which is of greatest concern to the non-industrial state—tends to be concentrated in a few world centres where the product exchanges are located and the financial resources for the credit apparatus are to be found. But of possibly greater importance is the fact that the great states are themselves the great markets and this affects the position of developed and under-developed nations alike. There are certain advantages in this, as has been suggested: there is a great saving in sales machinery and procedure where a single great market dominates. Nevertheless, the sensitivity of the exporting nation to the condition of that single market will be intense and the chances of managing to balance poor sales in one market with improved sales in another are likely to be slim. Moreover, this dependence will generally be intensified by the fact that the great states are at the same time the principal sources of development capital.

One of many possible examples. The wood industry alone accounts for about three-quarters of all Finnish exports. No less than two-thirds was taken by the EEC countries in 1959 and one-third by the EFTA countries. But Finland was unable to find the capital to execute a much needed

[1] Michaely, op. cit., p. 25.

revamping of the industry out of its own resources. It was fortunate, however, in being able to receive a World Bank Loan of $37 million for that purpose.

While the principal difficulties of the small, primary product-exporting state are not qualitatively different in any marked degree from those of the larger members of that class, the fact that its *aggregate* resources are the smallest has a profound influence on its capacity to progress technologically, diversify and improve its products, and compensate for market fluctuations. For those that are not so fortunate as to possess an exportable primary product dependence on foreign economic assistance is well-nigh total. But even the fortunate face problems of great complexity and gravity for which no solutions are apparent at the present time.

Typically, the small under-developed nation with a substantial foreign trade will be producing a very limited range of goods for an even more limited number of customers. Frequently, there will be no more than two or three major cash crops and a single mineral product. There may be less. But neither cash crops nor (crude) mineral products can be easily replaced or modified from within the given territory, if at all; and there will often be other countries, similarly placed, which produce a commodity that is identical or nearly so. Coffee, rubber, sisal, palm oil, rice, hard timber, copper and tin are obvious examples, not to mention petroleum. The producers' marketing organizations, if any, are usually weaker than those of the buyers. The capacity of the various producing countries to act together has been decidedly less remarkable than that of the buyers to play one off against the other.[1] Only in times of unusual shortage and

[1] The formation of the Organization of Petroleum Exporting Countries (OPEC) followed recognition of this fact and the common desire of the states concerned to form a united front against the international oil companies. However, for reasons which lie partly in the state of the market (the heavy increase in proved world resources and Soviet oil exports *inter alia*), partly in differences of view between the members and partly in the uncertainty as to whether economic or political aims should dominate its affairs, OPEC has not been a great success thus far. Some observers believe that its greatest contribution has been the instruction of its own members in the intricacies of the oil industry itself, thus strengthening their hands in negotiation.

urgent, immediate demand for, e.g. certain strategic materials, is the balance likely to tip in favour of the producer. Normally, the reverse will be true. There must be a serious political consideration for a powerful buyer to put economic advantage aside.[1] Not unnaturally, this is unusual.

The state producing primary goods is rarely in a powerful position. On the contrary, its reliance on a small and inflexible range of commodities and its weak position in the market make it peculiarly sensitive to the two events that can bring about the most serious repercussions within its own borders: fluctuation in price and technological change. In Latin America since the Second World War the deterioration in the terms of trade has been so great as largely to nullify the benefits of the net inflow of foreign capital (including, at various periods, the net benefit of aid granted by the United States).[2] In Ghana, drops in the price of cocoa from £150 per ton to £112 in 1960–2 and to £93 in 1965 upset the basis of the national economic development plan.[3] In desperation, it was proposed to diversify Ghana crops by re-introducing rubber and other plantations and to withhold cocoa supplies until the price rose. But it would take a number of years to develop rubber as a commercial crop, and Ghana rubber would naturally be in competition with rubber from Malaya and Indonesia, and elsewhere.

The development of synthetic fibres suitable for twine (one of many examples of technological change), has caused social unrest in sisal-growing areas in Mexico and the prospect of possibly more profound consequences for Tanganyika where sisal is the chief export commodity. Cases of under-developed countries drawing over 80 per cent. of their export income from agricultural commodities— for which demand conditions tend to be unfavourable—are

---

[1] As in Britain's consideration for New Zealand's dairy products or, to a somewhat lesser extent, United States attempts to help Brazil out of its difficulties in the coffee industry.

[2] Cf. United Nations, *Towards a dynamic development policy for Latin America*, New York, 1963, p. 78, fn.

[3] *Economist*, 24 July 1965.

common. The prices of the manufactured goods these countries import vary much less and rarely fall to a significant degree. The disadvantages are on one side, the advantages on the other.

II

For purposes of further illustration and comparison a table (Table IV) has been drawn up. It is based on figures published in the United Nations *Yearbook of National Accounts Statistics*[1] and includes all states which (*a*) are sovereign and (*b*) submit statistics which permit straightforward comparison with each other. For this reason the Soviet Union and its allies have not been included: their figures are grouped under conceptual categories which differ from those of the majority of states. Nor have the majority of African and Middle Eastern states been included, either because they do not appear in the Yearbook, or because their national accounting is rudimentary or even, in some cases, partly meaningless in this context: the nonmonetary sector being the dominant element in the economy. It should also be emphasized that all the figures are *official*, i.e. essentially as submitted by the governments in question and therefore not of an equal standard of reliability.[2]

Except where indicated, population figures are estimates for 1962.[3] Employing the categories defined in the introduction, it will be seen from these figures that of the forty-five states listed, thirty-five are small powers.

Except where indicated, the national accounts figures are for 1962. They are expressed in terms of the national currency of each state, either in millions or milliards, as appropriate. (Since only the ratios matter, it would be confusing to convert to a single currency.) On the other hand, the Gross Domestic Product per capita per annum is expressed

---

[1] United Nations, Department of Economic and Social Affairs, Statistical Office, *Yearbook of National Accounts Statistics, 1963*, New York, 1964.

[2] Thus, in the Philippines, traffic in contraband goods in both directions constitutes a very heavy element of foreign trade; but official Philippine figures cannot be expected to cover what is illegal without distinguishing it from what is not.

[3] Taken from United Nations, *Demographic Yearbook, 1963*, New York, 1964.

TABLE IV

(1) Country	(2) Population in thousands	(3) GDP/capita in U.S. $	(4)$ GNP	(5)$ Imports (Goods and Services)	(6)$ Exports (Goods and Services)	(7)$ Imports surplus	(8)$ Total resources of economy (GNP + imports surplus)	(9) (7) as % of (8)	(10) (6) as % of (4)	(11) Imports surplus as % of all imports
Australia	10,705	1,416	7,732	1,286	1,227	59	7,791	0·76	15·9	4·6
Austria	7,128	871	186·6	45·4	45·9	-0·5	—	—	24·6	—
Belgium	9,221	1,215	637·2	220·9	217·2	3·5	640·7	0·55	34·1	1·6
Brazil	75,271	250*	2,363·6†	202·9	166·8	36·1	2,399·7	1·5	7·0	17·8
Burma	23,183	52	6,528	1,168	1,315	-147	—	—	20·1	—
Canada	18,600	1,807	40,359	8,129	7,987	142	40,501	0·35	19·8	1·7
Ceylon	10,442	129	6,782·5	2,068	1,976	92	6,874·5	1·3	29·1	4·5
Chile	8,029	409*	6,361	633	550	83	6,444	1·3	8·6	13·1
Colombia	14,769	301*	29,638†	4,626	3,993	633	30,271	2·1	13·5	13·7
Costa Rica	1,274	339	3,134·7	833·5	718·6	114·9	3,249·6	3·5	22·9	3·7
Cyprus	580	432	94·5	47·9	40·3	7·6	102·1	7·45	42·6	15·9
Denmark	4,654	1,390	50,852	16,440	14,793	1,647	52,499	3·14	29·8	10·0
Ecuador	4,596	178	15,390	2,942	2,897	45	15,435	0·29	18·8	1·5
Malaya, Fed. of	7,376	241	5,891†	2,358	2,783	-425	—	—	47·2	—
Finland	4,505	1,047	17,021	4,509	4,258	251	17,272	1·45	25·0	5·6
France	46,998	1,300	353·6	47·3	49·3	-2	—	—	13·9	—
Germany, Fed. Rep. of	54,061	1,349	355·1	62·5	66·6	-4·1	—	—	18·7	—
Ghana	7,148	193	530	144	121	23	553	4·16	22·8	16·0

Greece	8,451	394	117,643	24,564	11,907	12,657	130,300	9·7	10·1	51·5
Guatemala	4,017	—	698·5	151·0	130·3	20·7	719·2	2·87	18·6	13·7
Honduras	1,950	202	836·8	168·9	173·9	—5	—	—	20·8	—
Iceland	182	355	11,258	5,105	5,569	—464	811	—	49·5	17·4
Ireland	2,824	641	761	287	237	50	—	6·17	31·1	—
Israel	2,292	823	6,120	2,795	1,362	1,433	7,553	18·95	22·3	51·3
Italy	50,170	688	24,693	4,247	4,090	157	24,850	0·63	16·6	3·7
Japan	94,930	504	18,995·8	2,028·5	2,100·5	—72	—	—	11·1	—
Korea (South)	26,520	105*	281·5	59·2	184	40·8	322·3	12·7	6·5	68·9
Luxembourg	322	1,499	25,340‡	20,083	21,816	—1,733	—	—	86·1	—
Mexico	37,233	356	177,533	18,258	19,429	1,171	178,704	0·655	10·9	6·4
Morocco	12,360	150	10·31	2·49	2·13	0·36	10·67	3·37	20·6	14·4
Netherlands	11,797	1,003	47,550	22,630	23,080	—450	—	—	48·5	—
New Zealand	2,485	1,505	1,444	325	330	—5	—	—	22·8	—
Nicaragua	1,578	249*	2,914	832	730	102	3,016	3·38	25·1	12·2
Norway	3,639	1,316	37,771	15,656	14,792	864	38,635	2·24	39·2	5·5
Philippines	29,257	191*	14,835	3,047	3,081	—34	—	—	20·8	—
Portugal	8,971	279	78,279	18,848	14,675	4,173	82,452	5·06	18·8	22·1
South Africa	16,640	435	5,942	1,234	1,717	—483	—	—	28·9	—
Spain	30,817	322*	615·11†	52·7	707	—18	—	—	11·5	—
Sweden	7,562	1,703	75,272	19,230	19,000	230	75,502	0·3	25·3	1·2
Switzerland	5,660	1,740	46·3	14·3	13·1	1·2	47·5	2·52	28·3	8·4
Taiwan	11,327	115*	72,375	14,469	10,064	4,405	76,780	5·74	13·9	30·4
Thailand	27,995	93	58·5‡	10·7	10·9	—2	—	—	18·6	—
United Kingdom	53,441	1,288	28,184	5,588	5,445	143	28,327	·5	19·3	2·6
United States	186,656	2,691	556,180	23,969	25,447	—1,478	—	—	4·57	—
Venezuela	7,872	901	25,927	5,682	9,947	—4,265	—	—	38·4	—

§ = in millions or milliards of the national currency. * = 1958 figures. † = 1960 figures. ‡ = 1961 figures.

in U.S. dollars, as it is the absolute figure that must be compared.

Two ratios have been calculated, as follows:

(*a*) Column (9) compares the excess of imports over exports (if any) with the total resources of the economy considered as the sum of the GNP and the imports surplus. This serves as an indicator both of the day to day dependence of the economy on foreign resources and the economy's general dependence on foreign support for its development. This follows from the fact that the imports surplus will, in the last resort, express capital transfers, i.e. capital formation which does not derive from domestic sources.[1]

(*b*) Column (10) simply relates exports to GNP to indicate in a general way the role and scope of foreign trade in the economy in question and, by extension, something of the nation's built-in sensitivity to economic developments or pressure from abroad.

Taking the imports surplus–total resources ratio (Column (9)) first, it will be seen that with one exception all the nations with a fairly high percentage (over 1 per cent.) are small. The exception, Brazil, illustrates the fact that some of the difficulties besetting small states are found, for the reasons already stated, in large developing countries as well. In contrast, of the eleven small nations which had an *exports* surplus (or negative imports surplus), Venezuela and South Africa may be considered special cases by virtue of their oil and gold exports respectively, while Thailand and Burma—fortunate in their rice exports—are both of a low level of general development. The remaining seven states all maintain a very high level of foreign trade, as can be seen from column (10). Those with an exports surplus are no doubt in a marginally better position than those with a high imports surplus–total resources ratio. But their reliance on foreign markets is undiminished as is, for the most part, their

---

[1] Adapted from D. Patinkin, *The Israel Economy: The First Decade*, Falk Project, fourth report, Jerusalem, 1959, pp. 128–30.

consequent reliance in the long term on their foreign trading for the general development of their economies.

The second index indicates even more clearly the correlation between the size of a nation and its stake in international trade. Of the thirty-five small states only *two* export less than 10 per cent. of their GNP. Chile exports 8·7 per cent. and South Korea 6·55 per cent. Of these thirty-five no less than thirty export 15 per cent. and over, and sixteen export over 25 per cent. of their GNP. Only four of the sixteen are under-developed.

It may also be seen that only four of the twenty-one small *developed* states (employing the arbitrary $300 per capita dividing line) have an exports–GNP ratio of less than 20 per cent. Of these four, three (Chile, Colombia and Greece) are borderline cases between 'development' and 'under-development', while Australia is clearly a special case in view of the immense distances that separate it from its markets and suppliers and the consequent special attractions of internal trade within the Australian continent. While this would appear to confirm expectations that development brings extensive foreign trade in its wake, it does not of course necessarily follow that lack of development inhibits foreign trade as such. It is the level of foreign trade relative to the GNP that tends to be higher in developed states.

III

While economic considerations and pressures weigh heavily in favour of specialization, political, social, historical and military considerations—and mere inertia—tend to limit the trend. Certain key industries may be retained or established despite their being unprofitable and even where equivalent products can be purchased more cheaply abroad. This, of course, is in fact doubly uneconomic since the economic potential devoted to the particular industry could have been invested in a field where the state has a comparative advantage. But the economic penalties for maintaining, say, a domestic aviation or automobile industry may be thought outweighed by the political and military penalties for giving up one's own production and relying on someone else's. This problem besets all states, great industrial powers such as Britain and France no less than their minor sisters. But since the key parameter here is aggregate economic resources the problem hits the small state much harder than the large. It is, very broadly speaking, a function of size.

There are, of course, a great many short- and middle-term tactics which in an imperfect economic world the small power (particularly the industrial one) can adopt and apply to the fundamental task of keeping its head above water. It is assisted by the fact that many of the greater and middle powers require foreign trade too, even though they retain characteristic advantages in its pursuit. In certain circumstances the political interests of other powers may weigh more heavily with them than the purely economic and serve to mitigate discrepancies in strength in competition with smaller states. But the latter's continued progress and development cannot be expected to survive really harsh pressure from greater economic and political units. It can only be maintained, if at all, provided certain norms of international behaviour are maintained. Where the balance is upset and where the political, military, or, indeed, economic interests of the more powerful units or groupings run contrary to, and outweigh, the advantages of accommodation with the small power—in its isolation—its situation may be extremely difficult.

Thus, the small power's high degree of reliance on foreign markets and on foreign sources of supply, compounded by the special difficulties stemming from specialization in exports and from having to retain a comparatively higher degree of diversification in imports, makes it particularly vulnerable to economic pressures and, *a fortiori*, to economic sanctions and economic warfare. In principle, raw materials can be cut off, markets interdicted, critical goods denied it, and domestic unemployment hugely increased with relative ease. All this can be done to an extent and in a proportion greater by far than in the hypothetical case of such pressure being exercised against a larger sovereign unit. Indeed, the simplest and most effective weapon to employ against a small power is that of economic punishment, for in all situations short of outright military conflict the weakest spot in the small power's armour is the economic one. A particular attraction of this weapon—to those who propose to employ it—is that retaliation is practically ruled out by its sheer ineffectiveness. No doubt there are very exceptional cases—such as that of South Africa, particularly in its economic relations with Britain—where the consequences of striking at the small state's foreign trade would be severe for other powers as well. But such cases, apart from being highly untypical, do not invalidate the general proposition that the minor state stands to be injured proportionately more seriously and, posibly, more permanently than those which attempt to inflict the injury. Nor does economic pressure necessarily produce the desired political results. The essentil point is that it can be exerted—and with relative ease, if not impunity.[1]

Granted this fundamental structural disability, the actual dependence of a given small power on foreign economic factors may vary greatly both in extent and kind. It will depend on the volume of foreign trade relative to total economic activity, on the rate and level of economic development, on the chosen fields of specialization, on the variety and nature of the nation's domestic resources and the skill with which they are utilized, and similar factors which by their presence or absence modify the country's relative ability to supply stated needs from its own resources and to exercise control over its own economic affairs. A determined government, enjoying public support, can *alter* the accepted and prevailing balance between foreign and domestic trade very drastically. This was done in Switzerland during the Second World War with considerable success. The area of culti-

[1] This question will be discussed in greater detail in Chapter 5 below.

vated land was substantially increased; labour was specially
recruited to work it and also to make up for the gaps left by
mobilization for armed service; and the non-agrarian population was compelled to grow its own vegetables.[1] But this is
a policy for time of siege. It cannot but stunt the economy
as normally conceived and carry with it harmful long-term
consequences. In some cases such a scheme may not be
feasible at all.

Not all the difficulties outlined here are exclusively the
bane of the small power's existence. Many of the problems
of the under-developed power, in particular, have nothing to
do with, or are unaffected by, size. But those which confront
the small *developed* and consequently more or less industrialized and technologically endowed states are found within it
in greater intensity and with more frequency than in the
greater states. It follows that for the small under-developed
state, the road to greater strength through development
leads to a new set of problems. From these, short of a radical
political change in the identity and character of the state,
there appears to be no escape.[2] These difficulties may be
summarized under three heads:

(*a*) Absolute limitations of size.

(*b*) A high degree of vulnerability on both the supply and
the marketing sides due in the first place to a high
level of foreign trade relative to the economy as a
whole and, in the second place, to a high degree of
specialization.

(*c*) A high degree of incompatibility between economic

---

[1] See RIIA, *Survey of International Affairs, 1939–46*, 'The War and the Neutrals',
pp. 218–19.

[2] Since we are concerned with the problems faced by the small power unaided by
significant political, military or economic association with other states, the possibilities inherent in economic union are not relevant here. But mention might be
made of one example showing how the economic and the political and military
factors can be related in such a case. Over 50 per cent. of Switzerland's trade is with
the EEC and the balance of economic argument favours its adherence to the community. However, Switzerland's traditional and still valid policy of armed neutrality
requires a strong, though necessarily uneconomic agriculture to feed the nation in
case of war. Under EEC rules, once the customs barriers were down, Swiss agriculture would be in danger of collapse under the weight of cheap Italian produce.

and political/military requirements, subject to considerable variation from state to state.[1]

All these work to the detriment of the small power. Were economic forces allowed to play themselves out, were there no imperfections of market, for example, it is difficult to see how the small state could maintain its economic viability *and* political independence for long. Relatively few are free of the need for foreign loans and aid, subsidized food imports, military equipment granted free or at reduced prices, technical assistance and the like. Most such help amounts to capital transfer in one form or another. The reasons for granting it are transitory. The reasons for requiring and requesting it are not.

The net political effect of these disabilities is to divide the world—from the small power's point of view—into two sectors: the group of states with which it trades and from which it draws its essential supplies; and all the rest. It cannot but be enormously sensitive to the condition of its relations with the former, while with the latter it can afford a calmer approach. In the first case, the interaction between economic and political considerations is dominant and constant; in the second, political considerations are to the fore.

In such circumstances, when the good relations between the small power and its principal suppliers and customers are in question, independence of mind and policy may be thought a commodity altogether too costly for consumption. Much will depend on the character and purposes of the national leadership and the support the population grants them. In time of crisis and conflict these will be decisive.

---

[1] The problem of defence budgeting and organization will be dealt with separately in Chapter 4 below. But clearly the government of a tropical country with no mineral resources, but extensive arable land, would hesitate to follow the example of Sweden and specialize in metallurgical industries.

4

THE ALLOCATION OF RESOURCES
FOR NATIONAL DEFENCE

I

T H E question of what fraction of national resources will be devoted to defence is one with which all governments wrestle and for which there can be no simple answer even in individual cases, let alone broad classes of nations. A host of economic, social, administrative, technological, political and military problems converge at this point in a manner so intricate that solutions to any one aspect generally alter the terms of all the others. For the small unaligned state these problems are of such gravity and are so little amenable to practical solution that they are easily and rapidly reduced for successive governments to the fundamental question of whether the effort to maintain and develop an effective capability for national defence is not entirely beyond their means —and whether, in consequence the protection of a greater power should not be sought instead. Such an alternative may be resisted on sentimental or ideological grounds. It may be inconsistent with national security. Or again, the political and geographical circumstances may be such that there is no great power in the offing which is prepared to assume the responsibility. What is clear is that where it has been decided, for whatever reason, to proceed alone a very great economic and social effort will have been undertaken, one that is proportionately greater by far than for states with comparable political and strategic problems but greater material resources. Those small states which undertake the effort may therefore be fairly distinguished from those that do not, or need not. Certainly there are cases where to devote only minimal resources to national defence, allowing existing forces to atrophy in a state of growing obsolescence of equipment and techniques, may be not only an attractive but a reasonable and justifiable policy. But among the non-aligned such cases are rare and the risks inherent in such a policy may be great.

These risks do not derive simply from an inability to field large forces. They stem essentially from the fact that the small state, because it is small, has an exceptionally slim margin of safety or security—in terms of both space and time. Even where its area is large relative to population, its forces will be too limited to defend more than the vital centres of population and economic activity against an enemy of equal or greater strength. It can increase the margin of time somewhat by attempting to defend border regions, but in a sparsely settled country it will encounter great logistic difficulties if it does so and have to shoulder the risk that tactical error or defeat will open up the defenceless heart of the country to the enemy. So for such a state the safety margin of space is illusory. A small and densely settled country offers no margin at all, neither one of space nor one of time. Indeed, in neither case can there be any question of strategic withdrawal (as opposed to evacuation) in anything like the sense that the Chinese and the Russians practised it in the face of the Japanese and German invasions respectively, or the French after the failure of their initial offensive in 1914, or, for that matter, the British when they withdrew the Expeditionary Force from France in 1940.[1] In all these cases the territory still subject to national control was sufficient to sustain resistance and, moreover, to serve in principle as a base for an eventual change of the military balance. For the small state faced with a great opponent witdrawal, if it is at all possible, can signify at best removal of the forces to a defensive, mountainous redoubt. The Czechs were thinking along these lines in 1938 and the Swiss laid down plans for a *reduit national* in the Alps with meticulous care during the Second World War. Alternatively, resist-

---

[1] In the case of the French in 1940 it would seem to be the case that no single reverse was decisive; it was the collapse of leadership and morale that mattered.

ance by guerrilla forces may be substituted when fighting in regular formations becomes impossible. But either way, a single, major defeat by superior forces means abandonment of the most valued parts of the country—if not all of it—and the loss of any prospect of substantial counter-offensive leading to victory on the basis of the nation's own resources. In short, the loss of a major battle is the loss of a war. Any reversal of the decision must await developments over which the rump state has no influence or very little. Only a change in the fortunes of the victor power in another theatre of operations or the arrival of reinforcements from outside can alter the balance. Thus where a small and a great power are in conflict the relationship is assymetrical. The Russian reverses at the beginning of the Winter War with Finland *could* have been decisive in the limited sense that they might have affected the determination of the Soviet leadership to pursue the war to the end. They did not. In contrast, once the Russians had broken through the Mannerheim Line in the first fortnight of the renewed offensive of February 1940, the campaign was over. The Finnish leadership could only register the fact; there was no question of withdrawal to mount a new offensive. Similarly, the German campaign in Greece was judged as good as over once the German forces had crossed the Pindus mountains on 19 April 1941.[1] Significantly, it was over for the *Greeks*; for the British who were involved there too it was not. The great power, by virtue of great national territory and population, or else by virtue of political or imperial arrangements made well in advance, or simply by virtue of the greater forces it controls, can attempt to push the perimeter of conflict away from its vital centres of population and industry and agricultural supplies. The small power, in contrast, must await the enemy at the gates, at the outer limits of its vital centres—invariably so when it is alone. Defence in depth is not a viable strategy.[2]

---

[1] J. F. C. Fuller, *The Second World War*, 1948, p. 107.

[2] In alliance or association with another power the small state may appear on occasion to be conducting a species of defence in depth. This is one justification advanced for Australia's contributions to fighting in Korea, Malaysia and Viet-

RESOURCES FOR NATIONAL DEFENCE   61

It follows that what the small power has reason to fear most is strategic surprise—a war for which no preparations have been made, or one from an unexpected quarter. From such a war it is unlikely to recover. And the significance of this is that the military *potential* of the nation matters a good deal less than the ready military power immediately available at the outbreak of hostilities or at the advent of the crisis. In some respects the strategic problems facing the small power in conditions of conventional warfare are similar to those which would face all states in the event of nuclear war: there can be practically no recuperation from major defeat and very possibly none from major *attack* either. But perhaps the most instructive comparison is with great conventionally armed states.[1]

Before the development of nuclear weapons the great powers, with much spatial and temporal room for manœuvre, were able to work out and execute elaborate plans for the mobilization of their manpower and industrial potential *after* the outbreak of fighting and even in the teeth of great defeats in battle. In 1944 Germany was producing almost five times as many aircraft as it did in 1939 despite Allied strategic bombing.[2] Britain, Japan, Russia and the United States performed similar prodigies of industrial and military organization. But the margin of security which the great powers had—and still retain in many respects—by virtue of, and in rough proportion to, their physical size and political influence is reduced almost to nought in the case of the small state. The techniques of direction of labour, allocation of physical and financial resources and means of production, and similar measures for the mobilization of economic and human potential for war must be employed

Nam. In fact, the Australian contributions have never been large and no great attempt has been made to disguise the fact that a primary purpose underlying them has been the desire to cement the American alliance. The Australian defence line, if it is outside Australia at all, is in Washington, not Saigon.
[1] Cf. Chapter 9 for a discussion of the possible implications of acquisition of nuclear arms by small powers.
[2] *U.S. Strategic Bombing Survey, Overall Report*, Washington, 1945, cited in Klaus Knorr, *The War Potential of Nations*, Princeton, 1956, p. 132.

before the crisis or not at all. Of course, this may well be a wise policy for all states; but for the small one it is indispensable. Of all classes of nations it is the small powers which can least afford to improvise. And there is thus an unmistakable requirement to make a bold and explicit estimate of the nation's needs and resources, both physical and political, and to decide in good time what will be undertaken.

Unfortunately, there is a natural and direct relationship between the general economic disabilities outlined in the previous chapter and the problem of what fraction of total resources can be devoted to governmental purposes, and to national defence in particular, without incurring self-defeating injury to the economy. The smaller the aggregate resources of the state the less a given fraction of the Gross National Product will yield. The poorer the society the more difficult it will be to extract any given fraction and the greater will be the social and political difficulties that attend such attempts. If the expenditure is—or appears to be—unproductive and if relatively little of it is ploughed back into the home economy, the disincentives to assume it will be that much greater. In consequence, expenditure in support of external policy (e.g. on the diplomatic network, propaganda, foreign aid, defence, &c., &c.) poses particularly acute problems for a small state and expenditure on the military element of such support poses the greatest problems of all. A modern military establishment is extremely costly regardless of size. It can easily be made to appear wasteful and disproportionately large. Its contribution to the economy may be real, but is nonetheless marginal. The elements of risk and uncertainty that attach to it are very great. And at every stage of the making of defence policy the small state will find itself facing the international political implications of its decisions such that the greater its success in satisfying its purely military requirements the greater will be its subsequent dependence on foreign sources of equipment and technology. In other words, the attempt to secure the physical defences of the nation is liable to lead to a weakening of its political defences. The heart of the problem—and of the dilemma which faces the small state—is that it is becoming well-nigh impossible for a small power to maintain a modern (conventional) military establishment without compromising its political independence and freedom of manœuvre even within the customarily limited sphere of small power action, while the need for an effective military establishment as the pre-condition of independent action and autonomous decision remains as profound today as ever it was in the past.[1]

II

The independent, unaligned power which is nevertheless intent on developing and maintaining a modern defence establishment is faced at the outset, and then at every successive stage, with a set of practical problems which grow in relative insolubility as the size of the state diminishes. They may be grouped, loosely, under two heads:

(*a*) those posed by the nature of modern weapons; and
(*b*) those which arise out of the impossibility of maintaining a wholly autonomous defence industry.

The first category is the fundamental one; the second is consequent upon it. It is convenient to consider them in turn.

In the public services *other* than defence the level of expenditure at any given level of national income and social services is roughly proportional to the size of the nation.[2] If the weapons normally required today were similar to those in use fifty years ago—the rifle, the machine gun, conventional artillery, fairly simple field engineering tools and equipment—this might be true of defence expenditure as well, at any rate where land armies were concerned. The smallest army could be, for all practical purposes, a miniature replica of the largest. It is instructive to note that under the Treaties of Versailles and Saint Germain-en-Laye, the categories of arms that Germany and Austria were either

---

[1] Cf. Part II for a discussion of the role of military force in the external relations of small states.

[2] Cf. Alison M. Martin and W. A. Lewis, 'Patterns of Public Revenue and Expenditure', *The Manchester School*, September 1956.

permitted or prohibited from possessing were substantially the same.[1] Yet even fifty years ago none of this applied to naval forces and today the complexity, initial expense and indivisibility of major naval units is to be found equally in land and air armies. High class fighter aircraft are designed for use with (and useless without) elaborate and exceedingly costly radar facilities for warning and guidance. Armoured units cannot be effectively employed without almost equally sophisticated systems of control and communication. Each unit—each aircraft, tank, anti-aircraft gun or missile ramp— constitutes a vast investment in resources for production or purchase, for training of personnel, and for the ever broader periphery of supply, communications and maintenance facilities. Furthermore, the tactics evolved for the employment of these weapons and vehicles pre-supposes a minimum number of units, as do the purely logistic requirements—if the fighting formation is to be kept up to strength in the face of the predictable breakdowns and supply difficulties. To take the ultimate example, it is at least debatable whether there is any point at all in maintaining a single aircraft carrier when tactical and logistic requirements suggest two or even three as the minimum number. It can be argued that a single carrier in action will succeed in little more than defending itself and its immediate vicinity against attack. And it is beyond dispute that if one carrier is to be permanently at sea there must be at least one more to replace it when it is taking on major supplies or being dry-docked. It is therefore worth noting the magnitude of the expense entailed by the acquisition of a single such vessel and its relation to the total resources of a small state. Australia[2]—by no

---

[1] League of Nations, *Armaments Yearbook*, Geneva, 1936, pp. 926–45.

[2] The choice of examples in this study and particularly in the present chapter is naturally dictated to some degree by what information is publicly available, yet reliable. Australia is, today, anything but an unaligned power. Nevertheless, its geographical isolation compels it to consider its defence problems in a special light and, at the same time, reveals the fairly simple causal relationship that can obtain in such cases between the limits of autonomous military power and the national policy adopted. In any case, whatever can be adduced about Australia's *difficulties* should hold in yet more severe a form for a state which does not have the advantages of consistent support from the United States and Britain.

means a great military power—has a standing requirement for aircraft carriers in view of its geographical situation. But the cost of a modern 30,000 ton carrier is in the neighbourhood of £50–60 million without its aircraft. The aircraft would probably cost a like sum and perhaps more. Carrier, aircraft and escort ships together could thus easily account for half the Australian defence budget current at the time when the project was particularly discussed (£309 million in 1965-6). Moving away from this extreme case and at a substantially lower level of complexity and expense, one may find an entirely comparable burden in the Ghanaian decision to acquire a naval frigate.[1] Its cost would be £5 million—or about 40 per cent. of the Ghanaian annual defence budget at the time the decision was taken (£12·7 million in 1964–5). It is hardly surprising that the frigate was ordered on the basis that the United Kingdom offer a 90 per cent. credit. Similarly, Ghana's contract for two transport helicopters—two being the absolute minimum for the facility to be of any practical use and reliability—involved an expenditure of just under half a million pounds, still a very large figure if related to the total defence budget and the country's national income. The main point is that both Australia and Ghana, starting at different levels of tactical and technological requirements and sophistication, feel the need to acquire new facilities at a higher than customary level or make more efficient and efficacious such facilities as they have. Both are subject to a fairly general rule that at whatever stage the armed forces of the nation may be, their promotion to a higher tactical and technological level requires vast and successively greater expense.

This is what occurs even when the nominal function of the facility or weapon remains unchanged. The aircraft carrier of 1970 will be nothing like the carrier of 1950; the modern rifle is unlike the rifle of the late world war. The difficulty and expense of keeping level with technical improvement of

[1] The frigate was ordered during Dr. Nkrumah's Presidency. At the time of writing it is not clear whether the new régime will take delivery. Meanwhile, the frigate has been built and launched.

the components of basic weapons systems is very nearly as great as conversion to a new system. The British naval aircraft 'Sea Vixen', built to replace the 'Sea Venom', will cost seven times as much; while even a comparatively pedestrian infantry battalion of the British Rhine Army will cost six times as much to equip in 1968 as it did only five years before.[1] Clearly, the decision to renew an existing weapons system is hardly less grave than the decision to acquire a totally new one, say, replace artillery-based air defence by surface-to-air missiles.

Where the potential opponent is substantially greater in numbers and resources, the incentive to acquire and employ weapons of the highest quality will be correspondingly powerful and the military arguments in favour of so doing unanswerable. This has been the Swedish position since the end of the war and it is therefore worth noting the magnitude of the task they have set themselves, particularly in the field of air-defence which entails a very high degree of complexity and expense. To replace the existing system and provide the country with a new one on a par with anything found or likely to be set up elsewhere (within the limits of conventional weapons) 'System 37',[2] based on the 'Viggen' fighter aircraft has been evolved and is in process of establishment. The 'Viggen' was designed by Swedes to Swedish specifications as a jet aircraft which can be employed for a variety of purposes—a 'flying platform'. Eight hundred of these craft will be built and with the ground installations the system as a whole will cost an estimated $1,600 million. This figure may well rise in time, but even if it does not, it should be compared with the current annual defence budget of about $830 million which is, itself, over 18 per cent. of the total state budget and about 4·5 per cent. of GNP. If spread over twelve years, as planned, this single but important element

---

[1] *Economist*, 17 July 1965.

[2] Details on the 'Viggen' project have been collated principally from the following: *Aviation Week*, 5 April 1965; *Christian Science Monitor*, 16 June 1965; *Daily Telegraph*, 28 May 1965; *Financial Times*, 18 May 1965; *Guardian*, 13 May 1965; *Interavia*, February 1962 and November 1964; and *UN Statistical Yearbook, 1964*.

of Swedish defence will account for at least 0·7 per cent. of GNP each year.[1] It will be the biggest single industrial undertaking in Swedish history. (Yet it is worth noting that compared with very roughly comparable aircraft—the British planned, but cancelled, TSR-2 and the American F 111-A—the Viggen is cheap, costing about a third as much as the F 111-A.)[2]

Expenditure of this order of magnitude constitutes a heavier burden on the small economy than on the large; it is also heavier on the poor than on the affluent. In the small economy it diverts resources away from industries that might otherwise approach an optimum scale of production. The defence establishment is a great consumer of goods and services and by increasing the range of requirements it deepens and sharpens the economic disabilities outlined in the preceding chapter. Where the society and its economy are poor, then, clearly, a given absolute expense constitutes a greater burden than in a wealthier case. The lower the income level the greater is the proportion of necessities in it. But since the absolute or real yield of a given fraction of the GNP is less in a poor state than in a wealthy one, the probability is that its defence requirements—which normally have nothing to do with affluence—will be proportionately much greater.[3]

Accordingly, in all situations short of outright conflict, the modern defence establishment constitutes a source of

[1] At the end of 1966 it was decided to freeze defence expenditure and *inter alia* reduce the operational strength of the Swedish Air Force. At the time of writing it is not clear how this will affect the rate of progress of 'System 37'.

[2] The F 111-A was in 1965 thought likely to cost some $4·5 million each. The Viggen will probably cost about $1·5 million. There are, of course, significant differences between the two planes and a straightforward comparison cannot be anything but misleading. But the similarities are there too, and would appear sufficient to give an idea of what investment is required for such projects. The low cost of the Viggen has excited universal interest and admiration.

[3] Compare Sweden with Portugal. Portugal, with a GDP per capita of $279·00 per annum devoted 6 per cent. of its GNP to national defence in 1961. The yield was roughly $157 million. Sweden in the same year, with a GDP per capita of $1,703 per annum, devoted only 4·6 per cent. of GNP and provided its armed forces with the equivalent of $615 million. (Figures from *UN Yearbook of National Accounts Statistics, 1962*.)

weakness, an accentuation of the general vulnerability of the small state to external pressures and an aggravation of the structural economic disabilities which derive from the absolute limitations of the small state.

On the other hand the military requirement itself is clear. The small, unaligned power—at least in so far as it is involved in or anticipates conflict—has the most profound reasons for attempting to offset limited numbers, limited supplies and small room for manœuvre by acquiring weapons of the highest fire-power, mobility and operational efficiency and which are consequently of the highest complexity and cost. In many cases it must do this not merely to offset the basic disability of small numbers and limited resources, but to prevent the aggravation of that disability by falling behind in the arms race.

The dilemma that faces the small power faces other nations of greater strength too. But for the small power the difficulties are intensifying at a much higher rate. They amount to a choice between two very unsatisfactory policies. The state can either resign itself to the prospect of the growing obsolescence of its military establishment and adjust its national policy accordingly. Or else it can attempt to undertake the ever-increasing burden of new weapons in the knowledge that it can buy respite for a few years at most and that there is no assurance that it can perform the same trick again. Meanwhile its economy is weakened and it lays itself open to an additional class of political difficulties and vulnerabilities. Once the decision has been taken at a given stage it is, of course, extremely difficult to mitigate or reverse it at a later stage.

How great a source of weakness the defence establishment will be—putting the strategic grounds for maintaining it in the first place to one side—will clearly depend on the magnitude of the defence effort in relation to total economic resources. But it can be affected by the extent to which the essential supplies are drawn from domestic, rather than foreign, sources. As will be seen, it is today an absolute

impossibility for a small state to maintain an entirely autonomous defence industry. But in determining what it will
attempt to produce at home and what it will seek abroad the
defence authorities will be faced with a number of extremely
difficult dilemmas to resolve—even on the assumption that
the weapons they require are freely available. And once
again, the smaller the resources of the state the harsher are
the dilemmas.

Broadly speaking, there are two mutually exclusive sets
of considerations to take into account:

(*a*) The political and diplomatic obligations inherent in any
arms deal; dictates of secrecy; independence of easily
interdicted sources of supply; thought for the military
and economic advantages that lie in maintaining a
pool of skilled manpower; and the influence of defence
industry on other technology-oriented industries.

(*b*) The huge overhead investment which defence industry necessitates and which might otherwise be employed in the purchase of additional weapons; the
risk of having to make do with inferior products and
the advantages of selecting weapons from a number
that have been tried and tested elsewhere.

These considerations are to be weighed either as part of a
coherent national defence policy, or else as particular cases
arise. But such questions must be deliberated against the
background of the steadily increasing difficulty of maintaining a domestic defence industry in the first place. Four unmistakable and apparently ineluctable trends may be discerned: the rising prime cost and technical complexity of
high-grade weapons systems; the rising absolute and proportionate cost of research and development; the rising
optimum scale of production of modern weapons; and the
high element of risk and uncertainty that attaches to the
process of design, production and employment as a whole.
Research and development are, however, the key factors,
since there can be no autonomous production of modern
weapons without them.

R & D has a greater impact on, and role in, the defence industry than in any other. It has been calculated that in the United States expenditure on R & D (as a proportion of total sales) is at least six times as high in defence industry as in all U.S. industry, and over three times as high as even in such civil industries as instrument-making which are typically 'research-oriented'.[1] Furthermore, the expenditure on R & D as a proportion of all defence expenditure on high-grade weapons is rising steadily.[2] Research costs alone for the British TSR-2 fighter project were estimated at £300 million.[3] In the event, it was cancelled; and there are some authorities who believe that an independent project of this kind is even beyond the reach of Great Britain—with the third largest aviation industry in the world.[4]

In such circumstances as these it is hardly surprising that there are only two small states—the Netherlands and Sweden—with anything that can be fairly judged a modern and reasonably comprehensive aviation industry—one of the key fields in this context—as opposed to assembly facilities, parts production and similarly important, but essentially marginal activities. But in fact neither the Dutch Fokker company nor the Swedish SAAB company are wholly autonomous. And both are quite small by international standards.[5] Fokker relies on foreign firms to supply the engines for its outstanding civil aircraft, the 'Friendship'.[6] SAAB, which has been unusually successful in the military field, will produce an engine for the 'Viggen' which is a

[1] M. J. Peck and F. M. Scherer, *The Weapons Acquisition Process*, Boston, 1962, p. 25.
[2] Ibid., pp. 26–27.   [3] *Economist*, 6 February 1965.
[4] 'The real lesson of the TSR-2 story is simple—that we can no longer afford to go it alone in the development and production of sophisticated military air weapons systems.' Marshal of the RAF Sir John Slessor in a letter to the *Economist*, 24 April 1965.
[5] Fokker employs 5,000 and SAAB 8,000 employees in its aircraft division. It may be noted too, that a vast outlay, irrespective of size or success, is required in the aviation industry. One estimate puts it at £2,000 per employee per annum. (*Economist*, 26 June 1965.)
[6] And got into serious difficulties when the British Government, in August 1965, forbade the supply of Rolls-Royce engines for the 100 aircraft Indonesia had ordered from Fokker.

development of an American (Pratt and Whitney) design. The company also has important arrangements with the American Hughes Aircraft Corporation for the production of electronic and missile systems.[1] Nevertheless the effort in the R & D field required of SAAB and associated companies is very great, as may be inferred from the fact that 37 per cent. of all Swedish defence appropriations for the years 1964–72 are earmarked for expenditure on material and R & D on the 'Viggen' project alone.[2] It is only natural that the Swedes continue to purchase many weapons which have a similarly heavy research and development element from abroad.[3] There is clearly no question of extending even the partial autonomy to be found in the 'Viggen' project through the full range of high-grade defence equipment.

The great investment on research and development, the high prime cost of the weapons themselves, and the frequently complex production processes they require all put a heavy premium on large production series and give a great advantage to the large firm. What was indicated above on the general difficulties of the small state where it competes industrially with greater nations is true, *a fortiori*, of the defence industry.[4] So while there is nothing unusual or surprising in comparatively under-developed states maintaining an elementary defence industry (say, ammunition production and some assembly facilities)[5] there is a steady opting out of the race as one ascends the ladder of complexity and modernity (or 'sophistication'). The Swiss, who run a close

---

[1] *Financial Times*, 18 May 1965; *Time*, 30 April 1965.

[2] *Financial Times*, 18 May 1965.

[3] E.g., surface-to-air missiles.

[4] An indication of the clear correlation between the size of the firm and the technological grade of the weapon or other item of defence equipment may be seen from the following figures for 'small business' participation in defence industries in the United States. In the aircraft industry—a mere 2·6 per cent.; in electronics— 7·8 per cent.; in ammunition production—19 per cent.; in non-weapon industries such as textiles and construction—over 50 per cent. Peck and Scherer, op. cit., pp. 138–9. And cf. C. Salzmann, 'Progrès technologique et Recherche opérationnelle', *Revue de Défense Nationale*, Paris, October 1960.

[5] Cf. detailed figures in H. Roberts Coward, *Military Technology in Developing Countries*, Cambridge, Mass., 1964, passim.

second to the Swedes in their readiness to undertake a substantial defence effort and their ability to produce high-
grade weapons themselves, have developed a highly original
assault gun, are preparing to produce their own medium
tank, and have traditionally high quality artillery of their own.
But the major components of their arsenal are imported.
And in the interests of efficiency, they are not above rejecting
a home-designed weapon for a superior one produced
abroad.[1]

In short, for the small state a wholly or even predominantly autonomous supply of weapons and of the no less complex and expensive control and command systems on which
their proper functioning depends is out of the question.
Furthermore, the tendency must be for the locally designed
and produced elements to diminish as a proportion (expressed in terms of value) of the whole.[2] Nor does extension
of the market hold out much hope. All arms producers
aspire to increase their markets and production series to
offset the high R & D costs and other overheads and those
that can manipulate political arrangements in this politically
sensitive field will clearly do so and have a built-in advantage over those that cannot. The small, isolated or unaligned
state is thus under a double handicap. Its political leverage
is likely to be limited and at the same time its specifically
military requirements will be for a wider range of weapons
and facilities than in the case of a state which is integrated
in, and partially covered by, a broad alliance.

One of the problems that arise where weapons must be
drawn from foreign sources stems from the high probability
that they will not be fully suitable or appropriate to the
specific tactical needs of the nation in question. Weapons
are designed for carefully defined requirements and these

[1] After field tests, a Swedish A/T missile was chosen and a Swiss design rejected.
Revue Militaire Suisse, May 1965.
[2] American defence experts are said to have calculated that even their highly
industrialized NATO allies and such associated states as Japan—not all of which are
'small'— will have no choice but to purchase between a quarter and one-sixth of
their arms requirements from the United States in coming years. *Economist*, 17 July
1965.

requirements vary greatly. One of the advantages to the Swedes of the Viggen project (and incidentally one of the reasons why the Viggen is likely to be relatively cheap) is its conception wholly in terms of Swedish defence policy and strategy. A foreign aircraft would inevitably be designed with different needs in mind and therefore either be wastefully excessive in the tactical facilities it had to offer, or else need costly adjustment, or again, simply be less than satisfactory. One of the main elements of the much-publicized military and political scandal that erupted in Switzerland in 1964 over the discovery that the appropriation for 100 fighter planes of $192·5 million, approved in 1961, would have to be increased by $133·9 million, was precisely this. The aircraft in question, the French Mirage III, were to be produced in Switzerland under licence. Ultimately, it was reckoned, 300 would be required, although the original appropriation was only for 100. However, these aircraft had to be adapted, firstly for use on Swiss mountain-side airfields and hangars, and secondly, for the Swiss pilots who, being reservists like almost all other Swiss military personnel, and having only a few weeks' training each year, required a simpler electronic control system than the professional French pilots could manage.[1] These specifically Swiss requirements did not account for all the increase of nearly 70 per cent. in the estimated costs, but they undoubtedly represented a high proportion. And what is probably more significant, they led to appalling delays. The Swiss Air Force received its first Mirage in October 1965; the complete Mirage wing is not scheduled to be fully operational before late 1969.[2] By that time the otherwise excellent aircraft will be on their way to obsolescence.[3]

The second difficulty is that a state so placed cannot always obtain even an approximation to its requirements.

---

[1] *New York Times*, 16 October 1964.

[2] *Aviation Week*, 19 December 1966.

[3] The upshot of the scandal, apart from personnel changes, was the decision to require the Swiss Air Force to make do with such planes as could be produced under the original appropriation—no more than fifty-seven, in fact.

The reasons may be political or bound up with considerations of secrecy, as may have been the case when after years of reliance on the West for their military aircraft the Yugoslavs were refused permission to build British or French fighters under licence and, in 1964, turned to the Russians. Or the weapons may simply not be available because the producer nations' facilities are fully engaged in supplying their own forces and those of their allies. In 1951 the Swiss resolved on the purchase of 550 medium tanks and then found they were not to be had. As an interim measure they had to make do with 200 light AMX-13 French tanks which were far from meeting their requirements. As a fairly natural consequence it was then decided to produce a suitable tank at home.[1] Finally, the supplier country may wish to retain certain weapons in its own hands as a matter of general policy of retaining the military upper hand for itself or of simply refusing to part with techniques and information built up at great cost and likely to render considerable, even incalculable economic benefits. Such considerations do not apply solely in the obvious case of ABC weapons; and small allies can be faced with as firm a ban as non-aligned states.[2]

These difficulties may be offset to some degree by the need of all arms-producing countries to enlarge their markets. Where political inhibitions are not strong and where the buyer country's financial resources are adequate for the deal to be completed without credit arrangements, and lastly, where its requirements are for a product which is approaching obsolescence, there is likely to be great enthusiasm on all sides to conclude a deal. Saudi Arabia's decision at the end of 1964 to provide itself with a modern air-defence system aroused interest and activity in all three of the major

[1] *Revue Militaire Suisse*, May 1965.

[2] In September 1965 the Netherlands were refused technical information on the building of nuclear-powered submarines by the United States, though it was clear that the Dutch Navy had only conventional (not Polaris-type) armament in mind. *The Times*, 1 October 1965. It may not be irrelevant that the Dutch have 'a parallel interest in acquiring nuclear power for merchant ships'. Ibid.

western states.[1] But it is more typical for the enthusiasm to be attenuated by the increasing difficulty of the small powers to find the money and the consequent need to assist them with credit terms or grants. And since there is, in any case, an element of the arbitrary in all armaments pricing, the way is open to varying the price with the political advantages or disadvantages of the deal in question. Political and financial advantage can naturally be equally incompatible on the purchasing side. At one stage of its progress towards the acquisition of modern fighter aircraft the Lebanese Government was reported to have pointed out to the Americans that the Soviet Union had offered them MiG 21 planes for a third the price of the roughly equivalent Mirage offered by the French, and that unless the Americans could do better the Soviet offer would be accepted.[2]

The small, unaligned power that accepts the logic of its strategic situation and recognizes that it must maintain a defence establishment that is both large relative to the size of the nation and of high technological grade, must take its decisions in the context of these difficulties and problems. The subject as a whole has a very high element of uncertainty. The assessment of requirements is conditioned by the accuracy of the intelligence estimate. The development of weapons always involves the risk of technical and scientific errors of prediction and a project of newly completed design may be obsolescent before it enters production. Such errors can be astronomically expensive. If the small power in the situation we are discussing were in fact able to shop freely for its high-grade weapons, it would have a considerable advantage over those nations which see themselves impelled to engage in autonomous production. But it is rarely free, as has been seen; and, moreover, the higher the grade of the

[1] The Saudis were offered French Mirage fighters, British Lightnings, and American F-104's. Ultimately, they chose the Lightnings. They also ordered Provost jet trainers, Thunderbird surface-to-air missiles and a radar defence system from Britain and Hawk surface-to-air missiles from the United States. The total cost seems to have been just under £200 million, but this was only part of the full outlay on defence decided on at the time.

[2] *Al Jihad,* quoted in *Ha'aretz,* 20 April 1965.

weapons system the greater the difficulties it will experience in its attempt to purchase them. The more sophisticated the weapons system, the higher its value to the small state, but the more numerous the barriers to its acquisition—political, economic, and military. It is at this level, too, that the costs of research and development are likely to be highest and— to counter the dangers implicit in failure—the spread of projects must be greatest. Incapable of large-scale and widely spread R & D the small power must specialize. It must also conduct its projects and make its decisions in this field while suffering from the fundamental disadvantage of necessarily lacking the fullest possible technical and scientific information and the facilities for testing what information it does possess. It is consequently bound to remain several steps behind the greater powers in many fields, both in respect of the weapons systems it is acquiring and of those it is planning for. Thus it will very likely be chronologically behind the great powers, not only absolutely weaker.

Where the secret-scientific component of the weapon is highest and most highly valued, as in unconventional weapons, there the qualitative advantage of the great powers is likely to be greatest and the difficulties of the small powers, in so far as they desire such weapons, particularly pronounced. On the other hand it is these weapons that characteristically tend to offset the numerical disadvantages of small forces; and by extension they will be those that the great powers have most interest in keeping out of the hands of the small. It follows that independent development —in the hypothetical case of a small power wishing to acquire such weapons—is for all practical purposes unavoidable.

These dilemmas cannot be properly resolved. The requirement for ever greater fire-power, ever improved communications and control facilities and ever greater mobility is clear. For the poor state the modern defence establishment is out of reach; for the wealthier state it can only be obtained at the cost of great and ever increasing effort. This puts an

obvious premium on the employment of military and para-
military instruments of the least possible technological
content—where they may be relevant. Alternatively, the
penalties for remaining outside the political pack—or of
being refused permission to enter—are made to appear ever
more stark and clear. The condition of non-alignment or
neutrality or any of the other maverick situations in so far as
they are supported by modern arms must become progressively less tenable. The dependence on foreign sources
for supplies, training facilities, tactical advances and the
other myriad components of the weapons acquisition process increases; the absolute capacity to produce one's own or
acquire anyone else's weapons decreases. Such trends, if
they are maintained, cannot but lead to an accelerated erosion
of the small state's independence. Yet clearly, these are slow
processes extending over many years; and their progress
will be influenced by two factors: the dimensions of the
total defence effort by the state in question and the technological character of the weapons it proposes to employ.

III

How large a fraction of total national resources is devoted
to national defence depends, in the first instance, on two
essential parameters: the level of normal economic activity
and consumption (as may be expressed in terms of national
income per capita, for example), and the far less tangible
and measurable factor of will or intent. The wealthier the
society may be, the easier is the marginal addition to the
defence allocation. The greater the dedication, the stronger
the public support for the government—or, alternatively,
the greater the government's ability to compel the public to
do its bidding—the more can be siphoned off from private
consumption and related public services to defence. Where
the country is both great and wealthy and the will to increase the defence potential strong, very great resources can
be found for defence and the relative shares of civil and
defence expenditure can fluctuate enormously from year to

year. In 1930 the United States devoted a mere 1 per cent. of GNP to national security and 71 per cent. to personal consumption; in 1940 the respective figures were still 1 per cent. and 68 per cent.; in 1944, however, national security accounted for 46 per cent. of GNP and personal consumption had fallen to 49 per cent. though this latter figure was still at a very high level when compared with what obtained in unoccupied Europe at the time.[1] In the changed national and political circumstances after the war the United States has devoted between 7 and 15 per cent. of its GNP to national defence. The steadily expanding American economy has meant that the absolute allocation for defence can rise steadily without the proportions changing and that, on the other hand, provided private consumption remains more or less pegged, the proportion taken by defence can even be increased in step with rising national income without an increase of the burden on the public.

The American defence establishment can only be compared directly with that of the Soviet Union. It emerges that, since the assessed Soviet defence expenditure per capita is approximately half the American, while the national income per capita is about 38 per cent. of the American figure, the real burden on the Soviet citizen is substantially greater.[2] Before Stalin's death the Soviet defence figures, as a proportion of all resources, were very much higher, perhaps 25 per cent. of GNP instead of some 15 per cent. as is believed to be the case today.

Official and public readiness to devote manpower to defence is equally flexible, but obviously subject to different pressures and processes. Consider Australia. In 1914, out of a total population of some five million, there were 330,000 volunteers for military service. In the Second World War, at the peak, and out of a population of seven million there

---

[1] Charles J. Hitch and Roland N. McKean, *The Economics of Defense in the Nuclear Age*, Cambridge, Mass., 1960, pp. 39–40.

[2] See Pierre Roustide, 'Budget militaire et équilibre nationale', *Revue de Défense Nationale*, June 1963.

were 640,000 Australians in military service. But in the early 1960s the regular army numbered just over twenty thousand, and when, in 1963–4, Australian defence problems and policy were thoroughly reappraised it was only with great difficulty that conscription was re-enacted and the planned strength of the army raised to 37,000. On the other hand the recognition of the change in Australia's circumstances, the diminished effectiveness of Britain as a protecting power, the appearance of centres of conflict in relative proximity, the need to enliven the ANZUS Pact— these and other considerations had a marked effect on Australian defence *expenditure*. Until 1963 defence expenditure was almost stationary in absolute terms, while *civil* expenditure by the central government rose by roughly two-thirds and GNP by some 40 per cent. In 1962–3, the last year in which the defence budget remained largely unaffected by external changes, it amounted to about $450 million. From 1963 onwards a steady rise was instituted and by 1966–7 it is planned to spend $1,000 million or over twice as much in the space of only four years.[1] Australia will then be approaching the Swedish figure of between four and five per cent. of GNP devoted to national defence which was maintained for many years with great consistency until it was allowed to fall in 1967. Still, a rise of 1 per cent. of Australian GNP in defence allocations will only produce $190 million (1963 figures), or not quite enough, as has been noted, for a fully equipped aircraft carrier; while a rise of 1 per cent. in the United States GNP allocation for defence would produce $5,851 million.

'Defence expenditure' is certainly a very loose concept, interpreted and employed very differently in various countries. Official budget figures are rarely based on uniform concepts and are, in any case, subject to rules of secrecy that

[1] Figures derived from United Nations, *Yearbook of National Accounts Statistics, 1962*, and *Statistical Yearbook, 1964*; Shane Paltridge, 'Australia and the Defence of Southeast Asia', *Foreign Affairs*, October 1965; and *Financial Times*, 11 November 1964.

may render them not merely incorrect but deliberately misleading. For the small state, particularly, the element of
foreign assistance may be very great and the resultant
figures may appear at first incomprehensibly high. Precisely
the same phenomenon may be noted where oil revenues—
hardly a product of domestic economic effort—constitute a
permanent source of income in a currency easily used for
arms purchases. Furthermore, money may be used differently
in different states and so may manpower. A comparison of
nine independent states in the Middle East, all of which for
one reason or another make a substantial effort in the field
of defence, shows this very clearly, thus:

TABLE V

State	Average defence budget as % of GNP	Average defence expenditure per inhabitant	Average defence expenditure per member of Armed Forces
	%	$	$
Egypt	5·80	8·31	2,105
Iran	6·06	7·02	936
Iraq	7·80	14·92	1,516
Israel	8·20	83·04	2,950
Jordan	19·31	28·15	1,318
Kuwait	8·45	255·02	n.a.
Lebanon	2·66	9·31	1,763
Saudi Arabia	14·19	24·11	5,000
Syria	7·36	11·23	982

The first thing to be noted about these figures[1] is that the
best available measure of total effort, the percentage of GNP
rate, is generally higher here than is customary elsewhere.
In Western Europe, excluding France, Britain and West

[1] Taken from Coward, op. cit., Appendix II, 17, 18. It should be noted that
these figures are all derived from overt information over a period of years—late
fifties, early sixties. Some of them are clearly inaccurate, through no fault of the
compiler; but taken as a whole they show what orders of magnitude are involved. The true figures are probably somewhat higher in most cases, but there is
no way in which this can be properly established. In any case, such a correction
would only strengthen the argument that follows.

Germany, but including Italy, the rate is anything between two and five per cent. of GNP. Secondly, that except for Kuwait these are all relatively poor countries, some very poor indeed. Foreign subsidies are clearly reflected in what would otherwise be the astonishing Jordanian figure; and oil revenues in the cases of Iraq, Kuwait and Saudi Arabia. For the rest it would be extremely difficult and in some cases impossible to work out precisely what the various countries owe to foreign assistance in any of its many possible direct and indirect forms: direct grants, long-term credits, diverted civil aid, lower-than-market prices for armaments, and so forth. It is nevertheless evident that domestic effort in those countries which have no oil revenues, nor really substantial foreign aid is very great indeed. Compared with this kind of social and economic effort, the Swiss decision to cut down their air-defence programme when their rate of defence expenditure was in the neighbourhood of only 3 per cent. of GNP is a close reflection of the changing Swiss attitude to national defence.

It can thus be seen that while it is possible to infer something of the absolute capacity for defence potential and establishment from a consideration of the total resources of the society in question, nothing can be said with any finality about the limits of the relative defence effort that society may undertake. On the country, it would appear that at any given, customary level of expenditure and human effort it is possible to postulate a material increase, *provided* the authorities are so minded and the public accepts their dictate. The breaking point is consequently one that should be conceived of in moral and political terms, not material ones. Though there is, in principle, a material breaking point, the moral one is likely to be reached first and is therefore decisive. And because the total resources of a small state are small and its strategic situation requires a greater effort relative to its size than need be pursued by larger states, the morale and dedication to the national interests of government and governed must be of a very high order.

IV

Where material possibilities are limited, the technical alternatives narrowly defined and a high degree of risk and uncertainty obtain, clearly the human variables of acceptable burden and of technical (and of course political) ingenuity count for a great deal. However, the human element matters very greatly in another respect. The objective limits of the small state's resources are, by definition, narrow. Any attempt to increase the defence burden beyond a certain point[1]—except in dire emergency—must be counterproductive, though there is of course no simple interchangeability between guns and butter. Some forms of butter, say electronic consumer goods, require and encourage skills and industrial plant which are closely parallel to those required by the defence establishment. Still, the smaller the resources are, the more acute the problem must be. It follows that there is a very great incentive to increase absolute resources or, alternatively, to find ways of maximizing what is to hand. One obvious possibility is to embark on a thorough prospection of geological resources, to accelerate the introduction of new industrial and agricultural methods of production, and to intensify the use of new synthetic materials and fuels where those found in nature are in short supply. Here, however, the small power suffers from the characteristic economic difficulties already described, needs great resources of capital which it is unlikely to have, and has no special advantage over larger states which can do the same with less effort and greater prospect of success. The problem is essentially economic; the military and political consequences flow from it.

[1] No attempt will be made to hazard a figure—which can only emerge from the examination of a particular case. But it would appear that for a prosperous, industrialized state, defence expenditure at the rate of 5 per cent. of GNP is not really burdensome and that it can be increased and even doubled without catastrophe even in times of peace. The problem is that heavy defence expenditure cuts down the rate of economic growth and so, by extension, limits the absolute value of a given fraction of the GNP at any particular time in the future. The political requirements of the state and the estimate of the potential opponent's policy must decide where the line will be drawn.

A second possibility is to seek a political arrangement to cure the economic weakness. It has been a fairly consistent purpose of Egyptian policy since the 1952 revolution to obtain a larger share in the benefits from Arab oil resources by one means or another. For a country with very slender resources and a highly ambitious national policy, such a policy—a distinctive form of 'neo-colonialism'—has obvious attractions. Other examples can be adduced[1]—but the essential point is that the great power, even where it lacks important natural resources as Britain and Japan do, has compensating factors in its very size.[2] On the whole, however, national purposes of this kind have a limited chance of success. If frontiers and governments solidify in the less stable areas of the world aggressive ambitions will probably cease to be practical politics.[3]

This leaves the third and most important possibility—making the most of one's manpower. Ostensibly, the small state would not seem to have an advantage here. In fact, there is evidence that where a small, but socially and economically developed society is concerned and where the public accepts the strategic and political necessity, more can be demanded of it than in larger societies with their lesser cohesion and stronger local, as opposed to national, loyalties. Sweden and Switzerland have the largest armies in Europe outside the Soviet Union; together with Israel, they show how the contradiction between the need to have very large forces available almost immediately to compensate for the narrow safety margin and the small absolute population figures and high defence costs can be largely squared. All three states rely on a very high degree of national loyalty, domestic tranquillity and professional competence on the part of their soldier-citizens.[4] The system has its limits and

---

[1] E.g., the Algerian–Moroccan conflict directly after Algeria's accession to independence and the Iraqi moves to annex Kuwait.

[2] Cf. Chapter 3, p. 41.

[3] This topic is discussed in detail in Chapter 7 below.

[4] The subject is very thoroughly discussed in M. R. D. Foot, *Men in Uniform*, 1961, pp. 60–81. A comment one might make on this otherwise very interesting

Switzerland is fortunate in not having to try to man naval vessels with short-term conscripts and reservists; its difficulties with modern fighter aircraft have already been mentioned.[1] It is nevertheless an important and distinctive solution which as a matter of historical fact great nations appear to be incapable or undesirous of except in periods of great and obvious emergency or tension—and then it is hardly distinguishable from total mobilization for war. For the small power, the citizen army constitutes a standing solution to a permanent problem of national security.

Where the requisite national cohesion, domestic tranquillity and discipline, minimal literacy and technical aptitudes and experience are not available—as is the case in most under-developed states—there the citizen army cannot be established. The alternatives are either to maintain a large, standing army which may be impossibly expensive and economically harmful, or else resignation to making do with a low proportion of the theoretically available strength. For this reason the inducement for a small under-developed power to compensate for its weakness by the acquisition of unconventional weapons begins to be felt at a much lower level of mobilized and mobilizable resources than in the case of a developed power of roughly the same class.

But more generally, the incapacity of the under-developed state to maintain a reserves-based army means it must undertake a greater economic effort than the developed power to achieve a given military product in the field. The relatively large standing army also automatically makes the military a more considerable element, socially and politically, than would be the case in an industrial society, and more in a small under-developed state than in a large one. For the small state is driven, in most cases, as has been seen, to mobilize or maintain in active reserve a higher proportion

book is that the author does not seem to give sufficient weight to the increasing difficulty of dealing with intricate modern equipment in 'citizen armies' and the consequent temptation to increase the element of regular personnel.

[1] See above on the Mirage affair. The Swedish Navy is largely regular and only part of the ships are in commission at any time; their air force pilots are all regulars.

of its population than the large one, irrespective of its level of development.

Two, more specifically political, consequences follow from the characteristically severe problems of defence organization and supply which the small power faces. Firstly, that so far as military procurement is concerned the small unaligned power has a built-in interest in the perpetuation of inter-bloc and great power rivalry. Rivalry increases the probability of finding a supplier for the required arms and eases the search for a new supplier when, as may well happen, political considerations cloud the relationship with the original source. Security would thus lie to some extent in the multiplicity of rivalries—commercial as well as political and strategic—within the class of major suppliers. Indeed, since great power conflict is itself a source of the impulse to produce (and hence, as has been noted, to market) weapons, reduced tension in the major fields of conflict might adversely affect the small power's facilities for acquiring high-grade weapons. For, clearly, not all small power defence efforts are functions of, or responses to, major power policy. There is a similar built-in interest, so far as defence procurement is concerned, in polycentrism, as opposed to the tendency towards bi-polarity, in general international relations. The greater the absolute number of producers and suppliers of weapons and related technologies, the easier is the small power's position.

Secondly, the almost unavoidable and certainly unambiguous dependence of the small state on those with greater and more elaborate defence industries, together with the steadily spiralling absolute expense and complexity of modern weapons systems, suggest that a limit to the grounding of national independence on military power is in the making. It would not be a finite, unequivocal limit and it would be absurd to try to predict precisely under what circumstances it will be reached or approached in any given case. But the tendency is there and the states in question all seem to be approaching it, somewhat in the manner that a mathematical function may approach infinity without reaching it—infinity being, by definition, out of reach. Sovereignty cannot be entirely eroded by a process, but its exercise can become progressively more difficult.

All this puts up the human and material price of national independence very greatly. And it also puts a premium on strength of will and the capacity to devise new tactics and take hard decisions in difficult circumstances. These difficulties—when and if they must be faced—contribute greatly to the cooling of the enthusiasm for rigorously upheld sovereign status and help to explain why the national attitudes of many old and experienced states differ so greatly from those of new, weak powers that have not yet had to deal with the problem in anything like its full measure.

5

VULNERABILITY AND COERCION

I

T H E measure of state power is the capacity of a government
to induce other states—or governments—to follow lines of
conduct or policy which they might otherwise not pursue;
alternatively, it is the capacity to withstand the pressure of
other states—or governments—which are intent on deflect-
ing it from a course which the national interest—or the
interests of its leaders—would appear to require. For the
great state it is the first aspect of power that is of highest and
most immediate importance; for the small state it is the
second. It may also be said that what characterizes the middle power in this respect is its indeterminate position between the two. But in fact all nations—and governments—
may be in situations where the non-customary posture
dominates: the small state may seek to pursue an active
policy, which is to say, one which implies a deliberate
attempt to alter the relationship between it and other states
to its own advantage; and great states in conflict with their
equals, or being bitten, like the fleas in the rhyme, by their
lesser brethren, may find themselves on the defensive.
Nevertheless, it is the peculiar and characteristic quality of
the external affairs of the small state that fundamentally,
and in the long run, it leads a defensive life. Its major problems are how to avoid situations where its weaknesses will
be exposed and exploited and how, on the other hand, to
make the most of its limited resources. The two problems
are closely connected.

An attempt to deflect a state from its settled policy may
rest on argument alone. It may be no more than a conven-

tional diplomatic effort to alter policy by altering the intellectual basis of its formulation—by bringing fresh information to the attention of the target government, for example, or by persuading it to reassess the consequences of its actions, or by subjecting its members to mental stress of sufficient intensity to alter their perceptions and judgment. Very occasionally even moral aspects of the issue at hand will be invoked—as when the Czech leaders in the period immediately preceding Munich were repeatedly reminded by the British and French representatives in Prague that responsibility for war, in the event of their refusal to accede to German demands, would be theirs. Yet unless the new considerations which the target government is being pressed to adopt have some demonstrable basis in reality such purely dialectical diplomacy must remain a very uncertain instrument of state. Where, on the contrary, it is within the power of the active party to the dispute effectively to alter the environmental circumstances of the target state—to create the material justification of the argument, as it were—there its diplomacy will be very powerful indeed. The coercion of one state by another consists, for all practical purposes, in just this: either in mounting a convincing threat to introduce or eliminate some element of importance into or from the other state's total circumstances such that the new environment will be manifestly injurious or insupportable; or in the actual and deliberate alteration of the target state's circumstances coupled to a promise to restore the *status quo ante* should certain conditions be fulfilled. By the same token, vulnerability to coercion consists in the state's circumstances being subject to manipulation by another power in this way.

The most obvious and best understood forms of coercion and vulnerability are, of course, the military. Some of the implications for war of the absolute weakness of small states will be considered in Part II of this study. The present chapter is concerned with non-military forms, those which imply injury by deprivation, rather than by destructive force, and specifically with much the most important of the non-forcible forms of coercion—economic pressure. To this the small power—and particularly the small power alone and devoid of assured external assistance—is peculiarly vulnerable.

We have already seen how the effort to expand and improve the economic and military resources of the small state leads almost ineluctably to a widening of the state's exposure to external pressure and interference. And this has suggested, in turn, that in practice the small power must distinguish sharply between those states with which it trades and from which it draws material and intellectual nourishment and those with which its relations are principally on the political plane. There may certainly be circumstances where it would have much to fear from conflict with the latter class—in the long run. But in the short run such conflict is likely to lead to decisive results only where it is unrestrained, in other words takes a military or quasi-military form. A whole range of possibilities for good and evil is eliminated where there is no significant trade and flow of capital between states. And in consequence, where the danger of physical conflict is remote—for geographical reasons, or because of the general political circumstances at the time—the sensitivity of even the smallest states to quarrels with their great, nominal enemies is likely to be small. This accounts not only for the reserve which many unaligned Afro-Asian states evince in their attitude to Cold War politics, but also for the manner in which the effective interest of the minor member states of NATO, CENTO and SEATO in their respective treaty organizations waxes and wanes from time to time and for the lack of conviction with which most Latin American leaders approach issues of world-wide significance as opposed to the very real feeling they invest in their multitudinous conflicts with the United States.

In contrast, the approach to relations with trading partners and supplier nations tends to be unaffected by distance and by transitory political developments. In fact, for the small state these relations constitute the fundamental frame of reference for all its external affairs—short of war. And conflict between it and its partners need not be acute to be serious.

The small state's susceptibility to pressure on its markets and sources of supplies is a function of its economic disabilities. Some greater states—such as Britain and Japan—share something of this susceptibility, as they share some of the disabilities. But this is rare. Moreover they have compensating strength in other respects. A great state, however precarious its economy, is itself a great market. It can and, indeed, invariably does have a periphery of economic dependents of its own. In the most famous attempt to institute economic pressure against a major power—against Italy in 1935—at least two small states were successfully inhibited from adhering to the League's decisions by their economic dependence on Italy. Italy was Austria's second most important market and was, moreover, heavily in debt to Austria at the time. Hungary exported 13 per cent. of all its exports to Italy, including no less than 52 per cent. of its surplus wheat. In contrast, only 2·4 per cent. of Italy's total exports went to Austria and 2·5 per cent. to Hungary. It is extremely rare, if not impossible, for a small state to attain this kind of regional economic paramountcy.

Coercion that is founded on the exploitation of economic vulnerability need not be put into full effect or even spelled out explicitly in diplomatic contacts for the desired political result to be produced. Economic pressure must be distinguished from economic warfare. While the latter, over and above the political intention underlying it, is designed to create lasting havoc and injury, the former is specifically aimed at the achievement of an immediate and limited political purpose. It will often suffice for the target state to be aware of it as a possibility permanently latent in its relationship with major trading partners. In consequence, the desired political effect may occur without any clear break with diplomatic, let alone economic norms. Much of

the relations, and more especially the tensions, between the
United States and the Latin American states rests on such
a more or less unstated and barely specified set of possibilities
which are nonetheless noted by all and feared or exploited
as the case may be.[1] So though there may be nothing in
principle to prevent a Latin American government from
'severing itself from the policy of common hemispheric
defence', there is, in the recurring American official view,
no moral or legal reason why the United States 'should not
be free to consult her own independent national interests in
giving or withholding any aid she may be providing by
grant or loans, or in reviewing any measures she may have
taken to stabilize or assist markets for her neighbours' products'.[2] In fact, in Latin America, more blatantly than elsewhere, but by no means uniquely, the latent penalties for
divergence from the existing diplomatic pattern and for
breaking free from the accepted limits of independent action, generally suffice to prevent the divergence from taking
place. Economic vulnerability is thus a powerful influence on
the *minds* of the leaders of small states, inhibiting recourse
to policies which might otherwise be adopted. Therein lies
its principal value for the greater powers.

It is worth noting, however, that the exercise of political
influence by economic means may produce a countervailing
political reaction. The United States has reason to use its
economic power in Latin America with care. As in the case
of warfare, the sane and cautious statesman prefers to profit
from the deterrent effect of his weapons, rather than employ
them in earnest. Yet there is nothing illicit about the em-

---

[1] 'In the present age most of the states of Latin America, and all the states of the
Caribbean area, are dependent upon the United States both in the field of trade and
in the sense that they hope for a considerable importation of American capital—of
course on their own terms. The formation of régimes antagonistic to the United
States is qualified by this important fact.' Dexter Perkins, *A History of the Monroe
Doctrine*, 1960, p. 389. For a passionate but sufficiently symptomatic Latin
American view of the relationship, see J. J. Arévalo, *The Shark and the Sardines*,
New York, 1961.

[2] Adolph A. Berle, *Latin America—Diplomacy and Reality*, New York, 1962, p.
80.

ployment of economic weapons as there is, nominally, about the employment of instruments of war. Employed unilaterally by one state against another economic pressure amounts to a set of acts which are essentially within the jurisdiction of the state: the institution of an embargo on exports or the denial of access to domestic markets, for example. It could probably be argued that any form of coercion is contrary to the Purpose of the United Nations Charter which enjoins 'friendly relations among nations';[1] but there is nothing more specific than that in the Charter and, clearly, it would be absurd to expect an attempt to outlaw all means of realizing the power potential of great states (as a major step towards genuine—as opposed to legal—equality with the smaller powers) to succeed at the present time. Still, it is undeniable that the improvement in international communications, the multiplication of international organizations and arenas of discussion and the publicity that attends their proceedings all serve to reduce the incidence of economic coercion and tend either to restrict it to cases where the political reasons for employing it are thought compelling, or at least to encourage the active party to proceed with maximum care and secrecy.

All this makes it exceptionally difficult to adduce hard evidence on this subject, or indeed to formulate valid generalizations on the processes involved. Evidence tends to accumulate only after the bubble has burst, when, in effect, latent, standing or initial pressures have been resisted or proved unavailing or when counter-pressure is exercised—as may occur in the case of a neutral caught between two belligerents. Normally, much remains unspoken and documents generally reveal less about the fears of consequences than about the consequences themselves when and if they occur. Furthermore, the topic as a whole is sometimes clouded over with conventional wisdom and unexamined

---

[1] Article 1, section 2: 'To develop friendly relations among nations based on respect for the principle of equal rights and self-determination of peoples and to take other appropriate measures to strengthen universal peace.' ('Purpose' is deliberately capitalized in the text of the Charter.)

postulates. When Uruguay was being pressed by the Germans in December 1939 to permit the *Graf Spee* an extension of its time-limit for refuge in Montevideo harbour, its spokesman told the Germans that seventy-two hours was the most they could grant 'without courting economic suicide'[1] as a result of British pressure for the ship's departure. British pressure was certainly very strong,[2] but Britain was not then or at any time during the war anxious to antagonize a generally friendly state, the economic ties with which were doubly important in wartime.[3] In any case, British pressure and objections to the extension of the time-limit were 'more technical than real'[4] as the naval force outside was still in no position to deal with the *Graf Spee* had it left and sought battle. The point here is that it was useful for the Uruguayans to argue the danger of economic penalties and that the Germans seem to have accepted the argument without demur and without further examination or thought.[5]

In the present chapter the two principal forms of non-forcible coercion—general economic pressure and interdiction of strategic supplies—to which small states are particularly vulnerable will be discussed and the circumstances under which they are most likely to be effective will be considered. It should be borne in mind, however, that the fact that a state is demonstrably vulnerable to some form of pressure is no more a guarantee that it will ultimately suc-

---

[1] *Documents on German Foreign Policy*, Series D, viii, p. 544.
[2] State Department, *Foreign Relations of the United States, 1939*, v, p. 102.
[3] W. N. Medlicott, *The Economic Blockade*, i, 1952, p. 461.
[4] Captain S. W. Roskill, *The War at Sea, 1939-45*, i, 1954, p. 120. (The Germans thought reinforcements had arrived and the decision to scuttle the ship hinged on their incorrect intelligence. *Documents on German Foreign Policy*, D., viii, pp. 542 and 544.)
[5] The British Minister in Montevideo may have hinted at economic penalties, but it seems highly unlikely that he went much further. The published documents suggest that his central argument was legal, which would have been appropriate in view of the common Latin American receptivity to juridical points. Cf. *Uruguayan Blue Book, Documents relating to the sinking of the Admiral Graf Spee, etc.* (London) 1940.

cumb to it than relative weakness in military strength implies the certainty of defeat in war. On the other hand, a marked discrepancy in strength—real or apparent—cannot but affect the initial approach to conflict of the parties to the dispute, marginally encouraging one side and marginally deterring the other.

11. *General Economic Pressure*

The government of a modern state has two faces. To the external world it presents itself, once recognized as legitimate, as a corporate body whose authority cannot openly be questioned, whose decisions and internal processes are privileged, and whose actions in the external sphere are, within very broad limits indeed, unbound by law. But in the domestic sphere it confronts the governed with nothing like this old-fashioned, somewhat mystical, semi-divine conception of authority—except possibly, and to a limited degree, in those countries where political or religious totalitarianism obtains, as in China or Saudi Arabia. Elsewhere, overwhelmingly and increasingly, the conceptual distinction between the state and those who rule it is well understood. So while it may be treasonable and reprehensible to act against the former, it is legitimate—at least morally—to question the utility, efficacy and authority of the latter and to seek to remove them. In consequence, it becomes the major and essential function of the group in power, the body of men who at any given time act in the name of the state and manipulate its machinery, to maintain the nexus between it and them. And to maintain it intact.

Because in their *external* aspect the body of men who operate the state machine are, by custom, assimilated into the state, a foreign move to weaken their domestic authority or interfere with the link between them and the machine runs against the grain of all peaceful and proper international relations. Yet where one government desires to impose its wishes on another and has exhausted those means which are commonly permissible within the framework of orderly relations, an obvious course is to consider action within the domestic sphere of the second government where it is both actually and conceptually more vulnerable. This is clearly illegitimate and many governments will be deterred by that fact, particularly where there is a risk of failure. But where there is a likelihood of success, the prospect may be inviting.

A crude form of such interposition between government and governed is, of course, subversion. It aims to weaken the internal strength of the government which is the object of the attack with a view to its replacement by another thought likely to adopt policies desired by the first government. Alternatively, it may be hoped that if the campaign is conducted with due care and efficiency, the very prospect or risk of such a replacement may in itself induce the object-government to re-think its course and quietly give way. However, unless the attacking government is pursuing a policy rooted in, and justified by, ideology, there is really no difference for its purposes—in this context—between a change of personalities in the leadership of the attacked state and a change of mind in the original group.

Economic pressure pursues essentially the same aim by attacking at the same point. Only its concrete means, and of course its ambiance, differ. It does not attack the government as such, it attacks the governed. By impoverishing them, or making their private lives difficult, or starving them, or reducing their comforts or their fortunes it may alter their attitude to their rulers, or to their policies, or both, and so upset the political arrangements within the state. That, at any rate, is the hope of those who employ economic pressure as a political instrument. If the mere fear that such changes in domestic political arrangements may supervene suffices, then, as in the case of subervsion and with much less ambivalence of intention the purpose of the operation will have been achieved.

Such an attack is not on the national economy as such. The impoverishment or permanent economic incapacitation of the state is not desired for itself, as it is in economic warfare, but is incidental to the question of policy which alone is in question. In practice there may be little difference, but so far as intention is concerned the distinction is clear-cut and important. The art of exploiting economic dis-abilities for political ends therefore rests on the ability to evoke sufficiently strong internal pressure or even to create a sufficiently powerful domestic force to operate as an *ad hoc* ally within the gates without doing so much damage to the economy that the relationship between the two states will be permanently altered.

Pressures exercised against the economy in the hope that they will duly be transmuted into political factors can be of very many kinds and occur in many forms. Among the possibilities are the closing of markets to the state's exports, denial of shipping and other transport facilities, blocking of accounts, freezing of credits, withdrawal of technical assist-ance, banning of investment by or in the state, embargoes on supply, prohibition of travel and communications—the list is a long one and the growing complexity of international trade and of the movement of capital tends to lengthen it. So does the steadily increasing economic dependence of the small states on the large already described. These and similar measures have this in common, that with very rare exceptions they are not available for use by the small states themselves. A small state may possess a contingent geo-graphical advantage. Egypt was able to deny Western Europe much of its regular oil supplies in 1956–7 with undoubted economic consequences for the European states affected. But this success owed everything to the accident of the Suez Canal passing through Egyptian territory (and the consequent ability to block it) and nothing at all to Egyptian economic strength. South Africa is therefore probably alone in its unusual power to dislocate the British economy—though this may be seen as the measure of the fragility of the British economy, rather than of the strength of the South African. And it is the unique quality of South Africa's economic strength—the gold component—that is the decisive factor, not its overall productive capacity. At all events, such rare exceptions apart, small powers are generally unable to inflict economic hardship on other states, certainly not on major powers. There is no effective legal recourse either. As already suggested, the state or states exerting pressure act wholly or principally within their domestic jurisdiction. Even if they are in breach of contract or treaty that fact alone will carry far less weight than the gravity of the political considerations which lie behind the measures taken and it is not difficult to find a justificatory reply to the inevitable protestations. It may be well-founded, technically. When Britain instituted economic sanctions against Hungary in 1935, as punishment for Hungarian support of Italy, the Hungarians argued that Britain was in breach of the most-favoured-nation clause of the economic agreement between the two countries. The British did not deny this, but simply replied that the United Kingdom was acting in compliance with a decision of the League of Nations. Or it may be a prevarication. When the Soviets stopped oil supplies to Israel at the outbreak of the Sinai campaign in 1956 and Israel duly protested, they argued that such commercial matters must be referred to court. So Israel was duly forced to sue a Soviet state corporation in a Soviet arbitration court and was subsequently turned down on grounds of *force majeure*,[1] the *force majeure* being the intervention of the Soviet political authority in the affairs of the Soviet oil corporation.

Except where the intention is largely one of demonstration and propaganda for the benefit of third parties (as in the case of Soviet oil sanctions against Israel or with the measures taken against Guinea by France in September 1958) the assumption must be, *ex hypothesi*, that the action will have the desired political result. Otherwise, the disturbance to the powers instituting the pressure, however slight, will have been unnecessary and the political obstacles to a settlement of the conflict by milder means multiplied. But

[1] Decision of the [Soviet] Foreign Trade Arbitration Commission, Case No. 16/1957, 19 June 1958.

economic pressure is very far from being a universally effective instrument of policy, despite the rather facile, yet still common belief that it is a valuable alternative to armed force and of almost equivalent potency.

The confidence in the efficacy of economic pressure, especially in the form of international sanctions, which still persists—particularly among leaders of the western world— was originally part of the Wilsonian creed. Lord Curzon gave it a classic formulation in June 1918, in the course of a general exposition on the coming world order and the League of Nations:

Then I come to the question of the sanction, which also, I think, must be somewhat closely scrutinized. The two forms suggested have been that of economic pressure, or boycott, and that of the use of force. In theory economic pressure is, of course, the easiest method to adopt, and it would seem *prima facie* to be likely to be the most effective. You suspend commercial intercourse with the offending nation; you stop her imports and her exports so far as you can; you prohibit communication by telegraph, by telephone, by post, by railway, by wireless telegraphy with her; you desist from lending her capital, or from payment of her debt; you blockade her coasts. Well, a good many of these expedients we have adopted; almost the whole of them we are practising in the present war. They did not, it is true, succeed in preventing the war; they have not, at any rate at present, curtailed its duration. But I should like to put it this way. I doubt very much whether, if Germany had anticipated when she plunged into war the consequences, commercial, financial, and otherwise, which would be entailed upon her by two, three, or four years of war, she would have been as eager to plunge in as she was.[1]

The confusion in Curzon's mind between the deterrent effect of impending economic sanctions and the effectiveness of economic blockade in wartime, and between economic warfare by belligerents and economic sanctions by the overwhelming majority of sovereign states is almost total. But it is nevertheless clear that, for the future at any rate, Curzon envisaged economic sanctions, or the threat of them,

[1] *Parliamentary Debates,* House of Lords, 26 June 1918, cols. 401–2.

as the rough equivalent, in more civilized times, of the despatch of gunboats and the landing of marines, to say nothing of full-scale war. A great deal of this confusion has lasted down to the present day.

Broadly speaking, and viewed within the context of the present discussion of economic pressure as an instrument of political coercion, the effectiveness of such pressure would appear to depend on five factors:

(a) The overall importance of the sector of the economy under attack.

(b) The availability of alternatives.

(c) The importance of the political issue at stake.

(d) The relations between government and governed.

(e) The tenacity with which each party pursues its course.

The value of a given sector of the economy and its contribution to the whole can only be usefully discussed in the specific terms of that economy. But any dislocation, as such, is costly. An existing pattern of trade and investment presupposes that it is the best available. And change that is more than marginal must therefore constitute an injury. One of the most difficult injuries to sustain is that which results from the loss of a major market or the attempt, of necessity, to enter and develop a new one. The more sudden the change, the greater the damage. Both Cuba and Egypt have discovered this to their cost in their efforts to shift their sales of sugar and cotton respectively to the new markets of the Communist Bloc. However, the key issue common to all cases is where the balance of advantage is thought to lie: with pursuit of the policy that has precipitated the attempt to exert economic pressure, or with the economic benefits which are held hostage, so to speak, by the dominant state or which are within its power to bestow.

In March 1954 the Organization of American States held its periodic conference at Caracas. It was marked by the clearest possible divergence of interest between the United States and the Latin American states. Secretary Dulles arrived with the single aim of inducing the Conference to

produce and approve what amounted to an extension of the
Monroe Doctrine aimed at communist infiltration into the
Western Hemisphere. The Latin Americans opposed this
purpose, disliked the spectacle of United States pressure on
Guatemala, were afraid that their formal approval of such
pressure would facilitate a new wave of North American
'interventionism', and were unimpressed by talk of communism. They, for their part, wanted United States
economic aid, assured prices for their exports, and long-
term investments of North American capital. And these
were only the head of a long list of requirements aimed at
easing Latin American economic dependence on the United
States and strengthening their domestic economies. At
first the United States delegation adopted fairly heavy
tactics, but when they saw how profound the Latin American
objection to the proposed anti-communist (or anti-Guate-
mala) resolution was they began to soften. An encouraging
prospect of general economic aid was dangled before the
delegates' eyes[1] and the hint of economic pressure seems to
have hovered in the background. Some Latin American
delegates readily conceded that if the United States 'acted
tough' it could push the resolution through in forty-eight
hours and that, generally, if the 'United States wanted to
badly enough, it could have the resolution passed declaring
that two and two are five'.[2] The Americans made only one
formal promise[3] and once Dulles had departed with his
resolution in his pocket and the conference got down to
semi-technical discussion of the economic issues, the United
States delegation became much less tractable than it had
been immediately before.[4] At all events, almost all the Latin
American delegations succumbed to the twin (alternative)
prospects of economic aid and economic pressure, conclud-

---

[1] *New York Times*, 5 March 1954.   [2] *New York Times*, 8 March 1954.

[3] That the US Export-Import Bank would start giving development loans once
more.

[4] *New York Times*, 19 March 1954. This was perhaps less a matter of deliberate
deceit than a symptom of the very real political (e.g. in Congress) and, to some extent,
ideological difficulties involved in a plan for US *Government* aid.

ing that they were in no position to stand their political ground when its economic price was likely to be so high. So while the Guatemalan Foreign Minister was warmly applauded and his bitterly anti-United States speeches were well received, most delegations voted against him.[1] Dulles sweetened the pill with a speech confessing that Latin American 'natural historical fears' of the United States were justified and reaffirming the principle of non-intervention in domestic affairs; and thus some honour was saved. But the fact remains that the United States got its way because it attached more importance to the immediate political requirement of a resolution of its own devising than to its long-term political position in Latin America, while the Latin Americans clearly attached less importance to standing their political ground than to the maintaining of their economic relations with the United States unimpaired and, if possible, improved. Latin American political hostility to the United States was, not unnaturally, hardened[2] and Guatemala was, of course, confirmed in its essentially rebellious fear of the North Americans. These, however, were effects of the kind that mature late, and opinion about their inherent importance, in Washington at any rate, was divided. The tactical victory of the Americans, such as it was, was complete.

Superficially, the difference between the political stand of the Latin Americans and their economic requirements may appear no more than that which is between a somewhat academic posture and very genuine and entirely objective needs. But there is no assurance that a position of political principle, no matter how academic or seeming unreasonable or impracticable or unjust, will invariably weigh less in the mind of the government concerned than nominally hard, economic facts.

This may be seen very clearly in the case of the economic pressure which Eire faced during the Second World War. In a general way its object was to inhibit the Irish Government from unrestrained pursuit of their policy of neutrality.

---

[1] *New York Times*, 8 March 1954.   [2] Cf. *Le Monde*, 30 March 1954.

It met with little success and when the questions of the bases required by the Allies on the Irish coast and the presence of Axis diplomats in Dublin became acute the possibility of greatly intensifying the pressure was discussed.[1] The Americans (once they had entered the war) greatly favoured this course. The British on the whole, were more cautious. There was never any question that had the Allies desired to injure the Irish economy they could have done so with ease and impunity. Ireland's dependence on the United Kingdom and on the United States for supplies, for markets, and as sources of foreign currency was extremely heavy. But nor, on the other hand, was there any serious doubt that the De Valera government would remain unmoved by economic sanctions and physically resist any forcible attempt to re-activate the bases once the economic sanctions had failed to achieve their purpose. The Irish armed forces were very small; there was no question of successful military resistance. But resistance there would have been, and the prospect of stirring up the Irish problem in all its complexity in the middle of the war was more than either Britain or the United States could comfortably face. The result was intense irritation,[2] but De Valera had his way in all essentials and Eire cleaved to neutrality with religious zeal to the end of the war.[3]

The Irish Government was successful in staving off the threat of economic sanctions because there was no conviction on the other side that sanctions would achieve their purpose. There appears to have been no question in anyone's mind that the Irish Government would be supported by the bulk of the population in the event of such measures being

---

[1] Cordell Hull, *Memoirs*, London, 1948, ii, p. 1355; Winston S. Churchill, *The Second World War*, London, 1950, iii, p. 641; R.I.I.A., *Survey of International Affairs, 1939–46, The War and the Neutrals*, pp. 248–52.

[2] 'If only he [Premier de Valera] would come out of the clouds and quit talking about the quarter of a million Irishmen ready to fight if they had the weapons, we would all have a higher regard for him', complained President Roosevelt. Hull, ibid.

[3] Except that towards the end of the war the Irish made a secret offer through intelligence channels to adopt security safeguards against espionage by Axis diplomats in Eire. Hull, ibid., p. 1359.

taken. The essential premise, that the pressure can in fact be successfully transmuted into political coin, was lacking. Furthermore, failure to move the Irish Government would have left the problems of the bases and the Axis diplomats unaffected, the prestige of the Allies at the height of the war would have been badly damaged, and there was always the possibility (which admittedly became more remote as the tide turned against Germany) that Eire receive external aid.

In this vital element of assured loyalty of the population in the exercise of national policy Eire and Israel have much in common. It is therefore interesting to compare the American pressure against Ireland, particularly in 1945, with that country's pressure against Israel in 1956 and early 1957, but particularly between 15 and 21 February 1957, when the United States considered and threatened to impose heavy economic sanctions on Israel if it did not evacuate the Gaza Strip. Economic support for Israel from United States Government funds had already been stopped at the outbreak of the Suez affair. Now, some $100 million of private investment and charitable support each year—according to an official American estimate—was in question.[1] In view of the probable domestic repercussions of such a step, a White House conference was held on the 20 February, attended by twenty-six Congressional leaders in addition to the President and the Cabinet members concerned. Senators Lyndon Johnson and William Knowland argued against the 'double standard' whereby no sanctions were asked for against the Soviet Union for a vastly more cruel and less justified flouting of a U.N. Resolution (over Hungary). But—

Ambassador Lodge replied that the United Nations would never attempt to apply sanctions against either Russia or the United States. This, he said, was just one of the facts of diplomatic life, because the territories and economies of each were so strong as to make them practically immune.[2]

[1] Dwight D. Eisenhower, *The White House Years*, ii, New York, 1965, pp. 185–7.

[2] Ibid., pp. 185–7. Cf. Herman Finer, *Dulles Over Suez*, 1964, pp. 475–87, for a passionate but by no means inaccurate account of the affair.

The Israel Government was far from immune, and after much soul-searching, gave way, having weighed the risk to its security entailed by the evacuation of Gaza against the injury to its economy implied in a loss of $100 million each year, to say nothing of the deeper implications of an intensification of its conflict with the United States. It was also clearly necessary to consider the effect on the country's security of so large an economic blood-letting, even though the conversion of such a loss into simple military terms could not be entirely straightforward.

It may be noted that for the United States the concrete question of whether Israel did or did not evacuate the Gaza Strip was of no direct importance—unlike the question of the Irish bases. It was the general, political posture of the United States in the Afro-Asian world and at the United Nations that was thought important and this could presumably be enhanced by the imposition of sanctions whether they achieved their ostensive purpose or not. So the United States did not have to examine too closely the probable reactions of the Israel Government. On the other hand, unlike the Irish, the Israelis were in much more severe conflict with a third party. American pressure on Jerusalem therefore had the effect, though doubtless not the deliberate intention, of reinforcing the Arab side militarily, economically and psychologically. For all these reasons the Israelis could not hope to deflect the Americans from their course in the very short run, and they had a clear and difficult choice to make. It is probably idle to speculate how long the sanctions would have been imposed and how severe they would have been had the Israel Government been prepared to defy the threat. What is important, in this context, is the relative weight attached to the political and economic issues before them by the Irish and the Israel Governments. It is these subjective assessments of the elements of the problem that lie at the heart of it.

Thus, in general, it may be seen that while the small power is in principle highly vulnerable to general economic pressure the successful application of such pressure requires a combination of circumstances that does not always obtain. Since coercion of this kind is in any case a function of close economic ties and these pre-suppose generally friendly relations—in the very recent past, if not the present—it is unlikely to be contemplated with any great frequency. It is as a permanent possibility that it matters most, always inhibiting the small power in its external relations, rarely precipitated except by the small power's divergence from the path desired by the major state. Yet clearly the probability of circumstances arising where such coercion may be considered, threatened or attempted increases with the degree of independence desired or insisted upon by the small state. For the unaligned small power it is therefore an extremely important element of its view of the external world.[1]

III. *Interdiction of Strategic Supplies*

There can be no absolute distinction, either in theory or practice, between pressures directed against the economy as a whole and attempts to deprive the state machinery of some specific and essential product or class of equipment. Economic pressures can be translated ultimately into security terms. Certain mineral resources, especially fuels, are no less essential to industry and agriculture than to armed forces. Nevertheless, there are sufficiently significant differences between the two classes of sanctions, boycotts, embargoes— or whatever other form such non-forcible pressures on the state, its population and its machinery may take—to justify considering them and their respective implications apart.

In the case of general economic sanctions or pressures, the logic of the action, as has been seen, is an interposition between governed and government, or the creation of a fissure within the government or some other source of

---

[1] Cf. Harold D. Lasswell's 'conception of power, using the term to designate relations in which severe deprivations are expected to follow the breach of a pattern of conduct'. H. D. Lasswell, *Power and Personality*, New York, 1948, p. 12.

opposition to the policy which precipitated the conflict. The measures themselves are necessarily broad and unselective in their scope. The probability of success is difficult to estimate.

Where the object of attack or pressure is the machinery of government itself or of some subsidiary or connected organism, the range of possibilities is very great, but the measures taken may be precise and limited in scope. An embargo on arms, ammunition or other military equipment, or on oil and other fuels, or attempts to prevent the purchase of essential and strategic raw materials or of certain classes of atomic fuels and other materials related to nuclear power, or the interdiction of technical information—all these are geared to an attempt to limit the power of the state in question and, above all, its actual or potential military power. Circumstances will dictate what is judged strategic.[1] It follows, that while the public may indeed rally round its government on general patriotic grounds, it is not itself under direct and immediate pressure. In this sense, and as compared with general economic pressure, the interdiction of strategic supplies is analogous to forms of limited warfare where only the fighting forces are engaged directly in the conflict and the civil population is, in principle, free to go about its business. Yet what distinguishes strategic interdiction from general economic pressure critically is that, while it strikes at the heart of the state machine, it is, on the whole, more easily parried. The resulting conflict is therefore likely to follow a different course with different ultimate political implications.

There are a number of reasons for this which may be briefly mentioned. Firstly, it is rarely impossible to find alternative sources of supply, provided the item under ban is sufficiently valued for a high price to be paid for it. Unlike

---

[1] In 1935, when sanctions against Italy were in progress, the British authorities in the Far East sought to prevent the Italians from obtaining not only materials of obvious strategic value such as tin and rubber, but even a certain root required for the production of insecticides. These were urgently required by the Italians in Ethiopia. *Daily Telegraph*, 28 December 1935.

the high cost of a general economic dislocation, the cost of a new source for a specific material or product is an incremental one, not unlike the result of a change in market conditions. Within the framework of the national economy, the money cost of the new source of supply is unlikely to be impossibly high. The cost in terms of time, transport difficulties, adjustment to new species of equipment and the possible political implications of the change are far greater and more significant.

Secondly, the goods and materials involved are generally of high specific value themselves. (Oil is an exception to the rule.) This makes deception a possible tactic. The goods may be transported through third countries, false manifests may be prepared, and the materials themselves may be outwardly disguised.

Thirdly, whereas the new arrangements that follow a general re-ordering of the economy's external ties are likely to be inherently unstable and unsatisfactory (as in the case of Cuban sugar, for which the United States remains the natural market) new arrangements for strategic supply may rapidly become both stable and permanent. In such circumstances, not only would the interdiction fail, but the possibilities of pressure latent in the original pattern of supply would be lost permanently.

Thus while, in the case of general economic pressure, it is all but impossible for the small power to retaliate effectively in kind, and extremely difficult to take counter-measures directed at the sanction itself, in the case of strategic interdiction the embargo or ban itself can, in principle, be countered or evaded. In this sense, the interdiction can be *resisted* and where resistance is likely the success of the enterprise will depend on the measures taken to render it ineffective. In consequence, no such interdiction can succeed unless it can be largely or perhaps entirely internationalized. This may mean an attempt to operate at source, that is, to gain the support and co-operation of all governments controlling sources of supply. American policy on the proliferation of nuclear weapons is based, explicitly, on the need to acquire the support of *all* governments in possession of the relevant techniques and materials for such a generalized embargo. Alternatively, where such interdiction at source is impossible, success will hinge on the feasibility of some form of blockade. But blockade implies the possibility of blockade-running, and, in certain circumstances, of armed clashes. In brief, the complexity, implications and risks of intensified conflict make the imposition of an effective interdiction difficult in all cases and tend to inhibit governments concerned from engaging in more than unilateral denial of supply. This would be a measure taken exclusively within the domestic jurisdiction of the state instituting the embargo and while it would thus avoid the difficulties, it would, by the same token, be relatively ineffective.

International support is clearly easiest to obtain where the major suppliers are not themselves involved in the conflict. Thus there was no real difficulty about instituting a general arms embargo during the later stages of the Chaco War between Paraguay and Bolivia in 1934. The great international arms producers who were members of the League, together with the United States and Japan who were not, all agreed on the embargo. However, though shortage of equipment and exhaustion of national resources played a considerable role in slowing down the war, the effect of the international embargo was somewhat vitiated by the fact that shipments through third parties did not cease,[1] and nothing prevented Argentina from supplying Paraguay with artillery shells from its own, unimpaired arsenals.[2]

The more important case (in the present context) is where one or more of the major suppliers is a party to the conflict and where, because the ban or boycott stems from its own power interests, the inducement to make it effective will be correspondingly great. For at least five years before the crisis in its relations with Guatemala in 1954 the United States

---

[1] R.I.I.A., *International Sanctions*, 1938, p. 30.
[2] David H. Zook, *The Conduct of the Chaco War*, New Haven, 1960, p. 193.

had refused to supply arms to that state. This had important domestic political consequences since, being starved of equipment from the traditional source, the Guatemalan Army officers were not unwilling to consider a new one. The United States Government went to great lengths to prevent the Guatemalan Army from getting arms of any description from any source. When the celebrated shipment of arms from Stettin arrived in Guatemala in April 1954, everything was done to prevent the new source from becoming a permanent one. Heavy pressure was put on western, seafaring states whose ships might be involved to permit the US Navy to stop and search their vessels and though most rejected the request, fairly effective unilateral action by the various governments was instituted.[1] Certainly, no second, major shipment got through in time to alter the balance between the Guatemalan loyalists and the CIA-sponsored invasion force or influence the deteriorating relations between the political leadership under Arbenz and the Guatemalan military commanders. The latter, having seen that the pro-communist policy was not going to yield a new supply of armaments after all, began to turn against Arbenz in earnest.[2] Had Guatemala had its own naval and merchant shipping facilities or had the Soviet Bloc been willing to employ its own ships, the American attempt to interdict supplies might well have failed. Alternatively, it would have changed the nature of the conflict greatly and increased its gravity.

Blockade is fundamentally a measure of war, but attempted interdiction of supplies may lead to its being considered. It has, for example, been promoted in the United Nations and by some writers on the subject as the necessary instrument for the 'non-forcible' coercion of South Africa

[1] *The Times*, 19 June 1954; *Daily Telegraph*, 18 June 1954; *The Times*, 15 June 1954; *New York Herald Tribune*, 10, 16 and 27 June 1954.
[2] See comments of British Minister in Guatemala in his dispatch of 26 July 1954, para. 11, printed in *Report on Events leading up to and arising out of the Change of Régime in Guatemala, 1954*, Cmnd. 9277, 1954. Cf. Ronald M. Schneider, *Communism in Guatemala, 1944–54*, New York, 1959, p. 301.

into abandoning *apartheid*.[1] As such it deserves to be mentioned here. In its most conservative form, this proposal calls for United Nations mandatory oil sanctions, assumes that they will not be universally respected and that suppliers will nevertheless be found, and argues that a naval blockade of the South African coast (and possibly the coasts of the adjacent Portuguese territories as well) is both necessary and sufficient. But even a rough and inevitably inaccurate estimate of the naval and logistic problems such a blockade would entail suggests that close to one hundred naval vessels, ranging from frigates to aircraft carriers, would be needed at any one time, not counting supply ships, tankers, communication vessels and the like. This immense force would itself consume some thousands of tons of fuel a day. One critical, but sober analysis of the plan suggests that the force would have to be kept in being for a year or eighteen months if it was to be effective and that the total cost might well be £180 million for such a period.[2] On the face of it, the prospect of such a sum being raised by the United Nations is unlikely; while the prospect of such a great force being recruited in the first place for such a purpose and for so long a period is unlikelier still. But the really difficult question is what happens if the South African Navy or Air Force are used to force the blockade, either by escorting tankers through the blockading ships and putting the onus of firing first on them, or else by direct attack on them. As with the Irish Government in 1943 and 1944, if it is generally believed that the South African Government will pursue its purposes to the bitter end and not hesitate to resist semi-forcible measures taken against it, the reluctance to undertake such measures in the first place will be correspondingly high.[3] At the same time, it follows that the first condition of

[1] Cf. Colin and Margaret Legum, *South Africa: Crisis for the West*, 1964; and some of the contributors to Ronald Segal (Ed.), *Sanctions Against South Africa*, 1964.

[2] 'South Africa: Oil is not the Answer' in *Africa 1964-5*, 18 December 1964. reprinted in *Survival*, March–April 1965.

[3] It may be that what some of the advocates of a blockade really want is to precipitate an armed crusade against South Africa, in which case their plan is self-consistent.

resistance to such a blockade of interdiction is the possession of appropriate military force of sufficient size and scope to inhibit, if not finally deter, any such project. The issue is then automatically carried into a realm where a great many other very grave considerations must be taken into account.

It would thus appear that two aspects of the question must be clearly separated: the availability of an alternative supplier on the one hand and the possibility of enforcement of the interdiction on the other. The latter aspect depends to a great extent on the tenacity of purpose of the parties in conflict, on their ingenuity, even on their daring, and to some extent on their logistic capabilities. In contrast, the former aspect—the availability of an alternative supplier—depends on a great many factors that are beyond the state's control. The essentials of the problem of military requirements have already been discussed.[1] The difficulties vary with the nature of the supplies that are required, the number of potential suppliers, the political relations between the state in question and the alternative suppliers and the political price, if any, that the state will have to pay the new source over and above the money price. Where the difficulties are potentially great and the security of the state machinery therefore held to be excessively fragile, there will, in principle, be a corresponding tendency to seek a higher degree of autarchy. The feasibility of the desired degree of autarchy sets one of the objective limitations on the freedom of manœuvre of the small power.

Interdiction of strategic supplies is therefore important chiefly as a possible bar to the pursuit of an active policy or, where the small power is in conflict with a third party, as a reinforcement of the opponent. It constitutes a weakening of an arm of the state, but no more. It is, therefore, in principle, and with due regard to particular circumstances, less grave in its consequences than general economic pressure.

[1] See Chapter 4 above.

IV

The vulnerability of the small power to pressure which exploits its heavy dependence on foreign trade and on foreign sources of strategic supplies is an inescapable consequence of limited economic resources. But this is not to say that in practice all small states need be equally concerned with the problem at any given level of aggregate resources and industrial development. Major and minor trading partners may be joined by common political interests of such importance to either side that no conflict or disagreement on any other matter between them would be allowed to jeopardize the *entente* or alliance. There may well be substantial political advantages to the major partner in clearly and publicly refraining from exploiting his economic strength. Contemporary views on political alignments require that they be entered into and maintained freely. As the experience of the United States in Latin America suggests, repeated attempts to keep the minor parties in alignment with the paramount state by the exercise of its coercive powers may be politically self-defeating, at any rate in the long run. Ever since the inauguration of the Good Neighbour Policy under Roosevelt, successive North American governments have oscillated between recognition of the futility of coercive policies and impatience to bring their Latin American partners to heel. Were the United States less intent on securing the cooperation of the Latin American states in realms—such as the Cold War—which have very little to do directly with inter-American relations themselves, it would be very much freer to employ its enormous economic strength to the full. And conversely, by supporting the United States in extra-continental matters, the Latin American States have generally succeeded in at least partially neutralizing the power of their major partner.

In contrast, the small power which remains outside a bloc of states or which pursues a policy which cannot be squared with its formal adherence to such a group, is in an exceptionally difficult position. Guatemala's cardinal sin (and Cuba's too) was to join rebellion against the United States to defection from the anti-Communist alliance—in a region where the former does not necessarily imply the latter. In consequence, the political value for the United States of retaining Guatemala's amity and co-operation was lost. Whatever temporary, conjunctional factors there may be to strengthen the position of the unaligned state *vis-à-vis* its dominant partner, they are always liable to rapid change and, at the very least, to severe re-evaluation by the dominant partner in the light of a divergence of interests. And this may lead in turn to an attempt by the major partner to exploit its inherent economic advantages to prevent divergence. It is true that, for all the reasons discussed, the exploitation of these advantages is neither simple nor necessarily successful, nor yet always politically wise. But the attempt may nevertheless be made and it is fairly clear that the small, isolated power can withstand such measures only at high cost and on condition of being blessed with a high degree of domestic harmony, unusual tenacity of purpose, and substantial material and financial reserves.

The success or failure of such attempts at coercion, given the will of the small power to resist them, are also much influenced by the factor of time: time for the measures to be instituted, time for emergency reserves to be gathered, time for the internal effects of the shortage to be felt, time for international co-operation to be marshalled, time for the vital element of shock first to be suffered, then to be overcome, and time for the act of embargo, boycott or other interdiction to produce its own effects and colour or alter the elements of the political situation which impelled one side to attempt coercion and the other to resist it.

There is, thus, no simple relationship between potential or paper economic power and its employment for a political purpose. For the major power it exists as a crude, uncertain instrument, permanently available for use where the necessary economic and supply relations obtain, but rarely appropriate in all respects to the tactical elements of the problem under consideration. For the small state that feels impelled to diverge from, or run counter to, the political requirements of the greater powers with which it is associated for economic or supply purposes such coercion must be seen as forever possible, a weapon forever suspended over it. But it can also be seen, not as something dreadful and unnatural, but, like the facts of geography, a permanent feature of the state's international environment, a permanent difficulty that successive governments must take in their stride. If this cannot be faced by the population and its leaders they have no practical alternative but to hope that no serious issue will arise to divide them from their major suppliers and trading partners (and the latter's allies) and to abandon the effort to pursue an independently conceived national policy when it does.

PART II

POSSIBILITIES

6

THE NATIONAL POLICY

AT this stage it may be useful to recapitulate, very briefly, to what conclusions the preceding discussion of the major facets of national strength and the conjoint ability to withstand external stress has led. Firstly, the weakest element of the small power's national strength is clearly the economic. Unlike the military or political elements, there is no prospect of even short term avoidance of all its long term implications. Nor is the difference between technologically advanced and retarded societies a crucial one for political purposes except in the limited sense that an under-developed society which has chosen to remain within the traditional framework of economic activity must be credited with a certain immunity to foreign pressure. But this is only the pauper's immunity to theft; in all other respects the under-developed state is highly vulnerable to interference—as will be seen. The really important point is that the advance to a higher economic and technological bracket intensifies and multiplies political difficulties and vulnerabilities and entirely fails to promise even an ultimate solution.

Secondly, because—as has been noted—there can be no autonomous recuperation from military defeat, the small power has good reason to seek to possess a substantial defence establishment well before the advent of unmistakable danger. Its margin of safety is too small for there to be any clear and satisfactory middle way between:
  (*a*) building up and maintaining a substantial and modern military establishment; and
  (*b*) reliance on political, psychological and legal factors and inhibitions alone.

The problem of the modern military establishment lies in the fact that its maintenance and renewal—and hence its effectiveness—are steadily receding as practical possibilities towards and beyond the limits of the small power's economic and social strength. Furthermore, the decision to make do with less than an effective military potential is, in effect, a decision to rely on political and other factors; and this decision is irreversible.

Thirdly, these processes cannot but weaken the capacity of the small power to withstand pressure or attack from its recognized opponents (where these are possessed of a more powerful economic base). At the same time they have made it peculiarly vulnerable to the pressures of those major powers with which it maintains close economic ties, founded though they may be on ostensibly amicable political relations. Indeed, it is possible to envisage circumstances where vulnerability to non-forcible pressure from nominally friendly powers may be many times greater than from unfriendly powers—not least because it may be more effective. At all events, it is clear that the unaligned power's freedom of manœuvre is subject to severe and growing restriction on all sides.

Fourthly, the mental climate in which matters of state are resolved by leaders of small powers is an inhibiting one. The decision to seek to overcome the objective obstacles to keeping one's position in the race—if only in the short term—is subjectively difficult. Special qualities of leadership, a special urgency of situation and, possibly, a particular quality of society and national culture may all be needed. But given such qualities and given a society which for historic and cultural reasons is amenable to great calls on its energy, resourcefulness and readiness for sacrifice, the small state may be endowed with political and military strength seemingly out of all proportion to its material resources. If anything, the relative simplicity of the small state's external and defence problems and the ease with which they may be reduced to the central question of national survival are in themselves great sources of strength. They can induce a siege mentality such as is relatively infrequent in the history of great powers.

Taken together, these are grounds for concluding that the condition of non-alignment is becoming progressively less tenable—and for technical and material reasons, not political ones. For some states in this class non-alignment is simply no longer commensurate with political independence in the sense that they cannot permit themselves any serious divergence from the lines of conduct demanded of them by the major states. For all states in this class situations may arise where external pressure—actual or potential—must lead to a re-definition of the national interest. This is to say, that where it is found that pursuit of the national interest implies conflict with major suppliers and trading partners such that the advantage in view would be offset by a very serious letting of economic blood and loss of strategic supplies, the effort may have to be abandoned. But for the small power, unlike the great, political and military margins are so slim that any substantial retreat or surrender involves the loss of some element of the basis or structure of national power or of the capacity to survive further conflict. Even when this is not in fact the case it may appear to be. Real or imagined, this is generally the question at issue for a small state in conflict with stronger forces, explaining much of the fierce Irish resistance to Anglo-American pressure for bases during the Second World War, for example, and the still fiercer Finnish resistance to the not entirely unreasonable or even—on the face of it—ungenerous Soviet demands for an exchange of territory put forward in 1938 and 1939. For leaders of a small state who find themselves with their backs to the wall it is difficult not to view any concession as the critical one making further demands both more likely and irresistible. The events preceding the Munich Agreement suggest that there may be good reason for such fears.[1]

[1] For a detailed discussion see: D. Vital, 'Czechoslovakia and the Powers, September 1938,' *Journal of Contemporary History*, October 1966.

It is for this reason that the capacity of a small power to withstand pressure—military in the first instance, but economic, political and psychological too—must be seen as the acid test of its viability as an independent state. In fact, increasing vulnerability to pressure and the progressive narrowing of the field of free manœuvre and choice which is consequent upon it render such viability questionable not only in the direct sense that they weaken the capacity to resist, but indirectly in that they affect the power of the state to alter its external environment to its own advantage and so retard or even reverse the processes enfeebling it. The viability of the small state which seeks to maintain political independence without the assured support of other and greater powers hinges, therefore, not only on its static capacity to withstand pressure or attack, but on its freedom to act in a positive way in the international arena with the object of increasing its material and political resources. It will be evident that even where such freedom of action is found it will be subject to quite narrow limits.

The external counterpart of the internal, absolute weakness of small states—their hall-mark—is the ease with which superior forces may be marshalled against them. The small power can hope to operate freely within the limits set by two points:

(*a*) the point at which it can safely maintain a defensive posture, i.e. effectively safeguard its status quo; and

(*b*) the point at which it is likely to evoke excessive, counter-productive response.

Where it ventures beyond the point of the degree of hostile response which it can safely contain, or falls back behind the point at which it can, with equal safety, contain the political, economic or military attack, it plainly loses the capacity to preserve either further freedom of political choice or, indeed, its national independence without recourse to outside help. It may survive; but its sovereignty will then be the gift of others, conditional on necessarily ephemeral international circumstances.

The first thing to be noted is the supreme importance of what might be called the *safe base*: the total national pool of economic and military, human and material resources over which the state has absolute and immediate control. Where the safe base is small and undeveloped, or inefficient, or unreliable the limitations on external action must generally be severe. The second point is that the practical problems that arise cannot be considered except in the context of the state's external environment and the degree to which that environment is receptive and amenable or, alternatively, hostile and resistant to its purposes.

It follows that within such limits the small state, however placed, has, in principle, the choice of three broad policies or strategies.

ONE. An essentially *passive* policy. The struggle to maintain freedom of choice in the external world is explicitly or implicitly renounced. The capacity to withstand conflict ceases to be a subject of serious concern—if it ever has been —either because no conflict is envisaged or because there is no belief in the ability of the nation to create a safe national base, or else because the social and economic price of such an effort is judged excessive and incommensurate with other social ends. This is a policy of renunciation. It implies acquiescence in the fact (or belief) that the state is not viable as an independent international entity. Nothing more need be said of it.

TWO. An *active* strategy designed to alter the external environment of the state to its advantage either by
 (*a*) reducing the discrepancy in strength between the state and the external forces that matter; or by
 (*b*) widening the limits of freedom of political choice and manœuvre; or else by
 (*c*) increasing the total resources of the state, and therefore strengthening the safe base by *external* increment.
Scope for the adoption and execution of such a strategy is clearly small.

THREE. A *defensive* strategy designed, in essence, to preserve the status quo, relying on strength through *internal* increment. In the short term this policy is subject to all the difficulties expanded on in previous chapters; but it is undoubtedly the safest, surest course to adopt where feasible. However, in the long term, given the evident pattern of economic and military difficulties mounting faster than the human and material national base can increase through internal growth, it appears to promise little for the future.

In part, the choice of policy will depend, as suggested, on objective factors: firstly, on the external, international environment; and secondly on the state's human and material resources, on the condition of the state's administrative and military machinery at the particular point in time, and on the ability of the leaders to marshal the national resources for political purposes. But it will depend, too, and perhaps more crucially, on the nature of the society in question, on the character and ambitions of the national leaders, and on the predominant view of the value and importance to be attached to the state as such—and even on the attitude to the future that lies beyond the period that can be foreseen with any clarity.

Thus the quality and ethos of the society very largely determine both whether the state can create and maintain a safe base, and for how long, and also what policy will be adopted. The quality and ethos of the *neighbouring* societies largely determine whether the conditions for a successful active strategy are present. For reasons which will be outlined further on, the states which tend to be impelled by internal considerations and encouraged by external circumstances to attempt the active strategy are to be found chiefly among the new states of Africa and the Middle East and, to a lesser extent, in the rest of Asia and in Latin America. Those which tend to cleave most notably to a defensive policy are the older states of Europe.

The two strategies will be considered in turn.

7

THE ACTIVE STRATEGY

I

I N an earlier era the impulsion to increase the resources of the state found an outlet in overseas colonialism or in the still simpler and older tactic of conquest and annexation of slices of neighbouring territory. Today, there are no territories left which are not formally part of a fully recognized sovereign state, while the formal sovereignty and integrity of states have acquired vast importance. The disinclination to upset so fundamental a convention of current international life is very strong and the small power is clearly the one least well placed to do so. However, it is the *formal* sovereignty of states which weighs so heavily and which is accorded so much conventional respect. So long as the forms are observed—or generally thought to be observed—respect for conventions can coexist quite easily with knowledge that they are subject to *de facto* violation. Even where public policy is traditionally and, on the whole, quite sincerely on the side of the maintenance and enforcement of international law and custom—as it is in the United States— principle is made to bow to national interest when the latter is sufficiently in evidence. The American Government has thought nothing of violating Cuban airspace (or indeed the airspace of any other country) when it thought this necessary: the dangers believed inherent in a hostile Cuba were judged to transcend the importance of maintaining active respect for international law. And there is no difficulty about adducing cases of such violations by other great powers in recent years. The really instructive point, however, is to be found in the fact that—taking the Cuban example again—the United States has been most reluctant to engage its own land or naval forces in any comparable action (such as reconnaissance), let alone give open material support for operations run against the Castro Government by covert means. This can almost certainly be put down to the fact that, until recently at least, the Cubans could do very little about high-flying reconnaissance aircraft and a great deal about hostile land and naval parties. As can be clearly seen in the light of the Bay of Pigs affair, effective Cuban resistance to American armed forces is likely to lead either to the ignominy of defeat or else to a widening of the conflict beyond the bounds of what is thought politically permissible. It is therefore the better part of wisdom to avoid committing national forces. Such political inhibitions are doubtless subject to change and, as both the Suez and Hungarian affairs of 1956 showed, where great powers believe their vital interests to be at stake, they may be set aside totally. But such events are rare and may become rarer still if the current inhibitions on the employment of violence by great powers which stem principally from the possession of nuclear arms take stronger root. However, given the common reluctance to cross this 'threshold', it can be seen that up to that point there is an essential relationship between the type and degree of *de facto* violation of sovereignty and the capacity of the state whose sovereign rights are in question to resist it. Moreover, while the *great powers'* freedom of action and choice of instrument is much restricted by considerations of global strategy, that of smaller, non-nuclear powers is not. And since, on the other hand, a great many of the new, small states are almost totally devoid of a capacity to resist encroachment, their weakness in the face of pressures exerted by their stronger neighbours is therefore, if anything, more serious at the present time than their weakness in the face of action by the great powers. It follows that here, in principle, lie opportunities for some small states to exploit their strength relative to weaker neighbours with a view to altering their external environment to their own advantage. Furthermore, this can be done by the exercise of national power.

The attraction of such opportunities is clear. The small, isolated state is not debarred from participating in political and commercial arrangements concluded between sovereign states on a basis of equality and joint interest. It has every reason to seek them. The difficulty is that it has little to offer. It is too small in size to offer security or military protection and too limited in resources to offer weighty commercial or financial advantages, let alone economic aid. Its ability to create or evoke an interest on the part of other states in friendship and co-operation with it need not be negligible in all circumstances, but it cannot be very great. Whatever it receives in return for political, economic or technical assistance will be subject to great uncertainties. It can make no arrangements which offer the class of security against stress that is inherent, in principle at least, in a fully-fledged alliance. In consequence, no freely negotiated advantage based on common interest can be reckoned an addition to the safe base of national power. A method less easily reversible is required if the material or political advantages which accrue are to be freely employable, fully or substantially subject to the control and manipulation of the state's leaders. To attain this the state requires at least the equivalent, though in a different form, of the great power's ability to coerce the smaller by non-violent means, such that the advantage is the product of power, not good-will. It is precisely this which the weakness of many of the new states of Africa and Asia, and to a lesser extent some of those of Latin America, make possible.

Three useful tests of the strength and effectiveness of a government are its ability to assert its authority throughout the national territory,[1] the degree to which that authority is readily accepted by the population, and its internal cohesion as a body. On all three scores a great many of the new states

---

[1] Also in international law. Cf. Hersch Lauterpacht, *Recognition in International Law*, 1947, pp. 7–12, 26–30.

are extremely weak. At the simplest level, this is a police problem. Scandinavia and Ireland apart, there are no countries in Europe with a density of population under sixty inhabitants per square kilometre. In Africa there are only three (Nigeria, Ruanda and Burundi) with a higher density; and in a great many it is far smaller, even less than ten. In Mauretania the density of population is *one*. And since the total populations of these very sparsely settled states is often very small too—Mauretania's population is approximately 800,000—it is to all intents and purposes beyond their power to maintain even symbolic control of their frontiers.[1] Genuine defence of the national frontiers against incursion is almost entirely ruled out. Where attempted, police and military dispositions and tactics must be akin to those of desert or even naval warfare and these clearly require a very high and expensive level of equipment, training and organization which are generally lacking and which, in certain cases, may be entirely unobtainable.

All this might not matter if the major ethnic, religious and linguistic groups were roughly coterminous with the political division of the continents into states. But, of course, there is no such correspondence. In the Middle East, with the possible exception of Saudi Arabia, there is not a single state which is not riven by deep ethnic or religious cleavages, often with a long history of mutual antagonism. Populations are composed of easily distinguishable and immiscible majorities and minorities, or there may be several communities and no majority at all. Many of the population groups spill over into other, neighbouring states. Iraq is traditionally ruled by the Arab Sunni minority; Sunni and Shiite Arabs together outnumber the powerful Kurdish minority; the Kurds are to be found in three of Iraq's four major neighbours—Turkey, Iran and Syria. In Africa and South East Asia there are comparable situations. The Bakongo are spread through both Congo republics and Angola, the Ewes through Ghana and Togo, the Somalis

[1] Figures from United Nations, *Statistical Yearbook, 1964,* New York, 1965.

through Somalia, Ethiopia and Kenya. In South East Asia the Shans of Burma, the Muslims of the Philippines, the Vietnamese of Cambodia and the Overseas Chinese throughout the area all have a strong communal identity and clear affinities with population groups in other states. Under stress, the communal loyalty may well count for more than loyalty to the state within which such groups reside and in whose governance they may or may not have a full share. A lack of congruence between the social fabric and the governance and boundaries of the new states is one reason for their internal weakness. The relation between power and office is another. To an extent unknown in older states, loss of office is loss not only of power over the apparatus of state, but of influence and prestige as well. Only those leaders whose political base is in the traditional framework of society and whose power stems entirely or substantially from extra-governmental sources—the tribe, the aristocracy, the plutocracy, organized religion and so forth—only they can face loss of office with a measure of equanimity and even some confidence in their capacity to survive politically. The modernist, nationalist politician may have the support of his community, at any rate for a time, but only rarely does he have natural, hierarchal authority within it. In so far as he is a modernist he must ultimately oppose the traditional hierarchy. Loss of office in the state apparatus is therefore loss of position and influence in his own community too. There being, as a rule, only one modernist political movement of any importance—the nationalist one—loss of control over it or influence in it leaves him devoid of all but two possibilities. He must either abandon political life or go into *disloyal* opposition. There is no other kind: either in principle—because the state and the sole strictly political movement are too closely identified; or in practice—because he is unlikely, for the reasons stated, to find useful and effective support within the formal limits of the nation. But because of the kinship and other affinities with groups across the border, it is possible to invoke their aid without serious qualms. There may even be a choice of patrons. The moral importance normally attributed to loyalty to legitimate government in the older nation-states has no precise equivalent. It is thus perfectly in character that an Iraqi Prime Minister should complain to an American Ambassador, complacently and without much heat, that the Syrian Populist and Nationalist leaders he had been subsidizing for years had proved unreliable because, it turned out, they had been offered bigger bribes by the Saudis.[1]

A divided population, many of whose components have close affinities with parallel groups in other states, is not necessarily a source of weakness and a minority, clearly, is not deserving of distrust merely because it is a minority. The political significance of these social and historic divisions hinges on whether or not they are taken up by foreign states and disaffection is encouraged and supported by subversive means. Where this is done—and done successfully—and the results turned to political profit by the foreign government, then the two states, the one which is subject and the one which is object, enter into a relationship which is a total negation of the principle of mutual respect for sovereign rights.

The seeking of popular support for one point of view or one form of leadership in countries other than one's own has fostered factionalism to a dangerous degree, splitting countries to the point of revolution. It is nothing but a new form of imperialism, the domination of one state by another.[2]

This is King Hussein's cautious comment on Egyptian subversion in Jordan. It is the heart of the matter.

II

The chief advantage of subversion as an instrument of national policy for small states is its economy of means.

[1] Waldemar J. Gallman, *Iraq Under General Nuri*, Baltimore, 1964, p. 163. The author was the United States Ambassador in Baghdad 1954-8.
[2] King Hussein, *Uneasy Lies the Head*, 1962, p. 75.

Here, contrary to what is usual in international conflict, the most violent forms are cheap—in both material and manpower—and the milder forms the more costly.

Given suitable operating terrain, land hunger, enemy injustices, etc., a hard core of thirty to fifty men is, in my opinion, enough to initiate armed revolutions in any Latin American country.[1]

Setting aside Guevara's major thesis, that the 'revolutionary situation' need not be awaited passively, but can be created,[2] this judgment can be shown to have considerable validity. For what he appears to have meant is that the long, painful process of peasant-based rebellion and guerrilla war can be set in motion and maintained by a handful of militants *provided* certain social and topographic conditions are met. The extraordinary possibilities inherent in subversive warfare—*modern* warfare in Roger Trinquier's telling phrase[3]— require only one more element; support from the outside. Where it is lacking, or intermittent, or subject to the uncertainties of very long lines of communication and transmission of supplies—as with the UPC in the Cameroons or the Hukbalahap in the Philippines—its effect is much reduced, almost to nuisance value. Some degree of foreign support is indispensable. Where the going is hard a great deal will be required, as the North Viet-Namese have not hesitated to recognize. Unlike classic revolutionary warfare, subversive warfare draws much of its momentum and justification, let alone its material needs, from such external support.[4] The two aspects of such warfare—internal revolution and conflict between states—must therefore be carefully

[1] Ernesto ('Ché') Guevara, 'Guerrilla Warfare', in Mao Tse-tung and Ché Guevara, *Guerrilla Warfare*, 1963, p. 147.
[2] Ibid., p. 111.
[3] Roger Trinquier, *La Guerre Moderne*, Paris, 1961.
[4] 'If the Vietnamese people's war of liberation ended in a glorious victory, it is because we did not fight alone, but with the *support of progressive peoples the world over, and more especially the peoples of the border countries, with the Soviet Union at the head*. The victory of the Vietnamese people cannot be divided from this support.' Vo Nguyen Giap, *People's War People's Army*, Hanoi, 1961, p. 36. (Italics in text.)

distinguished. As a system whereby internal revolution is initiated and sustained, by a foreign power for its own international, political purposes, subversive warfare can be a most efficient and economical tool.

The milder techniques—propaganda, financial support and the harbouring and boosting of exiles—tend to be more difficult to exercise and more costly, and to require a greater measure of tactical subtlety. Even so, none of this is beyond the bounds of any but the very poorest and weakest of states. Cuba broadcasts no less than 220 programme hours a week to foreign countries and Egypt 477; and so both compare very favourably with the Voice of America (873) and the BBC (639), *not* counting 'grey' and clandestine stations.[1] Considering that the geographic and linguistic range of Cuban and Egyptian propaganda broadcasts is much smaller than that of the VOA and the BBC, these are impressive figures.

A second advantage inherent in the subversive instrument is that the state which is the object of such attacks can counter them only with great difficulty, if at all. It cannot exploit the racial, communal or social affinity on which the subversive effort is based because its own prime concern is to minimize the divisions within its own camp and give the political frontier social as well as geographical significance. Internal weakness impels it to look inwards and attempt to heal domestic lesions before venturing abroad. 'Nous n'avons aucune revendication. Tout ce que nous demandons, c'est qu'ils restent tranquilles,' was the Emperor of Ethiopia's natural response when asked for his view of the perennial tensions between his country and Somalia.[2] The inflammatory broadcasts from Mogadiscio to Somali tribesmen in Ogaden, the introduction of arms and money among them, attacks on the Djibouti–Addis Ababa railway and the rest have had to be answered by measures taken on a quite

---

[1] Figures for 1965. Source: *BBC Handbook*, 1966. On Egyptian 'grey' or semiclandestine broadcasting ('Voice of Free Lebanon', etc.) see, for example, Joachim Joesten, *Nasser*, 1960, pp. 177–9.

[2] Interview by Jean-François Chauvel, *Le Figaro*, 4 March 1964.

different plane of activity: reinforcement of troops in the affected area, staff talks with Kenyan military leaders,[1] and —where the opponent was sufficiently out in the open—by military action. Retaliation in kind has been clearly out of the question. The difficulty about the conventional exercises in national power to which the Ethiopians have been restricted is that, however effective in themselves, they can be politically self-defeating. Each is evidence of the Somalis' power to deprive the Ethiopian Government of a measure of control over its territory and over many of its subjects. Each can be interpreted in Mogadiscio as progress towards the realization of the Greater Somalia project whereby Somali *terra irredenta* is to be incorporated into the national state. For other powers, the ability of the Somalis to sustain the conflict is an invitation to exploit it in their own interests at third hand: aid being channelled to the Somali authorities and ultimately transmitted to the rebels in the field.[2] However, quite apart from the question of Somalia's ultimate prospects, it is clear that its capacity to engage in subversive warfare against Ethiopia and Ethiopia's inability to operate beyond the bounds of conventional instruments of policy do much to reduce the disparity in military strength between the two states.[3] Somalia's reaction to its local military defeat at the hands of Ethiopian troops early in 1964 was—logically enough—an intensification of its propaganda campaign.

This discrepancy in conventional military strength is not unusual; it is one of the reasons for the attraction that subversion has for powers which are militarily inferior to the states with which they are in conflict. However, when employed by states which themselves possess the conventional military preponderance—as with Indonesia and Egypt, both of which are given to employing subversion as a normal

---

[1] Chauvel, ibid.

[2] On Egyptian support for Somali nationalism see Saadia Touval, *Somali Nationalism*, Cambridge, Mass., 1963; pp. 178–80.

[3] Ethiopia's defence budget is $18 million for 34,000 military and 29,000 police personnel; Somalia's budget is $3·9 million for 7,000 military and 4,800 police. Institute for Strategic Studies, *The African Military Balance*, August 1964.

instrument of policy—the situation of the state under attack is naturally made very much more difficult.

Finally, the attacking state—where it is unaligned and operating against another state of the same class—has greater freedom of action than if it limited itself to more conventional instruments of conflict. Unlike regular military assault, subversion by small powers does not evoke a high degree of automatic concern and hostility in the international community. In the first place, given non-alignment, it can rarely be immediately evident which of the extra-regional powers or power-blocs stand to gain by its employment, even if it were to lead to regional preponderance.

Secondly, subversion is readily visible to all who wish to see it, invisible or unproven to all who do not. It provides possibilities for endless prevarication, denial, washing of hands and counter-denunciation. Being covert it is not easy to provide firm evidence of its existence, let alone its detailed workings. Where evidence is available the means by which it was obtained may make its publication impossible, or at any rate render it suspect.

Thirdly, it is easily controlled. The dependence of the clients upon the patron is very great and funds, supplies and political assistance can be readily shut off or transferred to more promising candidates. Outlawed by their own government, they cannot permit themselves to quarrel too frequently with their masters unless, like the Syrian Populists, they find themselves new ones.

However, it follows that a government which proposes to employ so formidable, yet subtle, an instrument must itself possess a high degree of administrative ability. Decisions must be swift and rigorously executed. Internal authority must be very great. Funds must be made freely available for purposes which do not allow of formal accounting. Operators with all the necessary intuitive gifts for such work must be found. And, above all, the state must be made to appear strong and unyielding in its purposes, for otherwise the dissident elements will look elsewhere for support. Only very few of the new states possess the necessary combination of material and human capabilities on the one hand and ruthlessness of policy and ambition on the other to take advantage of the weaknesses of their neighbours in this manner.

III

Given these potentialities for establishing a measure of influence over, by interference in, the affairs of neighbouring states, what can be made to accrue in this manner to the sum of the nation's material and political resources? Subversion has been defined as 'the undermining or detachment of the loyalties of significant political and social groups within the victimized state and their transference, under ideal conditions, to the symbols and institutions of the aggressor.'[1] The first part of this definition is useful enough, but the second presupposes a degree of ideological motivation which, while it should not be excluded from the present context of the new states, is rare. The achievement of power, or the release from the power of others—this is what matters and it is for this that the 'aggressor' state provides the means: arms, money, international political backing, sanctuary and so forth. While such aid is given the subversive element is dependent upon it; a more complex relationship need not be posited and where it exists cannot be of great importance. Once the subversive element achieves power— *if* that is its purpose—it has within its grasp all the advantages, practical, political and psychological, of government. In consequence, its dependence on the 'aggressor' state is automatically and drastically reduced. The latter can only prevent this by repeating the process in other forms with fresh or modified subversive elements or else by concluding binding political arrangements—some form of pseudo-federation for example—immediately after the attainment of power and before the dependent group has had time to settle in and accustom itself to authority. However, experi-

---

[1] Paul W. Blackstock, *The Strategy of Subversion*, Chicago, 1964, p. 56.

ence in the Middle East and Africa in recent years has not been encouraging in this last respect.

Yet nothing so drastic as a full-scale transfer of power need be intended. It may be self-defeating, as already suggested, and much can be achieved without it. Subversion in its most fundamental and restricted sense of illicit interference in the domestic affairs of another state offers a better chance of achieving more modest aims.

The purpose of an active strategy, it has been suggested, is to alter the external environment in favour of the state by one or more of these three means: reducing an unfavourable discrepancy in strength, broadening the field of manœuvre and choice, and increasing the total resources on which the state can count in time of stress. Accordingly, there are two classes of targets: those which pertain to relations with the neighbouring states and those which pertain to relations with the extra-regional powers, the great states of the world. While subversion, where undertaken by a small power, can only be employed with reasonable safety against another small country, in its effects it can be brought to bear on both classes of targets: the first and third points principally concern the neighbouring small power, the second concerns the greater powers too through the agency of action against the smaller ones.

How Somalia has managed to reduce the discrepancy in effective power between it and Ethiopia has already been noted. A more ambitious and deliberate example is suggested by the evidence that in 1963 representatives of the Ghanaian African Affairs Centre were giving covert (financial) support to an oppositional group in Dahomey.

It had long been one of Nkrumah's more immediate objectives to form a union between Ghana and Dahomey which would have absorbed the Togoland strip in between whose independence he never recognised. Ghana would have dominated such a union, and thus found itself sharing a frontier with Nigeria, its great rival, and able, therefore, to give considerable aid and comfort to Mr. Awolowo's anti-Federal Action Group, just across the border. The Ewe tribes spanned these artificial frontiers along the coast, and were constantly used by the Ghana Government as anti-Nigerian spies.[1]

None of the long series of Dr. Nkrumah's interventions in the internal affairs of other African states—of which his assistance for Patrice Lumumba and his successors is perhaps the most publicized example—were strikingly successful in the sense that a lasting master-servant or even teacher-pupil relationship was established in any single case. President Nasser's efforts have been more durable, but even they have been subject to decline. But clear and unmistakable success is what subversion is unlikely to achieve. It suffices that its political benefits—enhanced prestige, nuisance value, reduction of the opponent's strength and freedom of manœuvre, maintenance of the political initiative, and the like—can be garnered over a limited period of time. The opposition that Dr. Nkrumah aroused in his time is more vocal than that which President Nasser has had to face, but there is very little of practical value that their opponents have been able to do about either. In the meantime—certainly up to his removal from power in Accra early in 1966—Dr. Nkrumah was able to retain a position and an influence over events that he would have lost long before had he relied on what would have been his due as leader of a state of some seven millions with a defence establishment costing no more than some $35 million per annum. Indeed, as with the economic pressures that certain great powers are in a position to exert on their small trading partners and customers, mere dread of such interference can suffice to produce results.[2] In short, subversion is a covert, indirect form of conflict and its fruits, for that reason, are liable to be somewhat uncertain and to lack the full and satisfying

[1] *Sunday Telegraph*, 8 March 1964. The witness is anonymous but described as having been in a position to know of these matters at first hand. Internal evidence supports this.

[2] It seems to be concern lest vulnerability to such interference be exploited, rather than fully documented reasons for believing that it is or will be, that largely accounts for the acute sensitivity of the Turkish Government to matters relating to its Kurdish minority, or that of the Philippine Government to its Moslems and Chinese.

flavour of older forms of imperialism. But they are none-theless real. Because they derive from the employment of the aggressor state's national power, not from good will and diplomatic exchange they are far more resistant to counter-pressure and to stress from the outside, even if they do require considerable gifts of patience and resilience in whoever proposes to enjoy them.

There has been no completely successful attempt to achieve permanent positive control of another state's mate-rial and human resources through these means, as distinct from reducing the forces—political, military and economic—that opponents can put into the field. The establishment of the United Arab Republic in 1958 was, perhaps, the closest approximation to such event. However, though the Egyp-tians duly attempted to enforce control over Syria while the Union lasted through a form of permanent interference in local, Damascus affairs—and ultimately lost their position there as a result when the Syrians revolted—their subversive activities in Syria *before* 1958 were only one of several factors softening up the Syrian state. Nevertheless, it would seem unreasonable to rule out future successes for such policies. The inequalities of wealth between the new states are very striking and much of the conflict between them can be put down to attempts to rectify what often appear—or are made to appear—gross and arbitrary injustices of distribution. Legal and historic arguments apart, Morocco's conflicts with Mauretania and Algeria, for example, both concern regions that are extraordinarily rich in mineral wealth. It is also arguable that had General Kassem moved either very much faster or else much more slowly and more adroitly than he did in June 1961, exploiting social tensions inside Kuwait instead of relying on military bluster, he might have succeeded in his attempt to establish a form of overlordship over the territory.[1]

---

[1] The Anglo-Kuwaiti Agreement granting full independence to Kuwait was published on 19 June 1961. The Iraqis waited until the 25 June before putting out their claim for integration of Kuwait in Iraq. The first British troops did not arrive

But such complete and formal control over an increment to the national resources is not essential, given the willingness to have the indirect benefits of such resources. This can come about in several ways: by inducing the victim state to buy off the aggressor with economic advantages: supplies, loans, communications facilities and the like; by inhibiting it from exploiting its own advantages to the full;[1] by impelling it to co-operate politically against a third party.[2]

So far as the great powers are concerned the purpose of an active policy must be the widening of the field of manœuvre in relations with them by the employment of an instrument of policy which is itself subject to close manipulation by the small power. Here too, subversion—where internal and external circumstances are propitious—offers some advantage so long as the great powers themselves continue to be inhibited from full exercise of the power available to them. In very broad terms there are two sets of possibilities. In a region where the influence of the great powers is uncertain or divided, as in most of Africa and the Middle East today, any act which enhances the local

until 1 July and the full protecting force was not in place until 7 July. Iraqi tanks did move down to the desert, but slowly and ineffectively. Had a group of Kuwait dissidents been prepared before Iraq moved—in the manner that the Egyptians operated in Lebanon and Jordan in 1958 without the benefits of a common frontier —there might have been a different *dénouement*. The bombastic military and diplomatic tactics adopted could not possibly have succeeded. Subversion, patiently and carefully executed, might have, and might yet do so.

[1] On the connection between Egyptian intrigue in Khartoum and Sudan's reluctant decision to compromise on distribution of the Nile waters and compensation for flooding of part of its territory on completion of the Aswan High Dam, see Tom Little, *High Dam at Aswan*, 1965, p. 64 et seq.

[2] For example: '. . . the request to discuss the future of the American airbase and the British forces in Libya springs not from a governmental conviction that as a nation whose national power is growing it is beneath its dignity to have foreign troops on its soil. It springs instead from the fact that the leaders of the government realize that growing social and political unrest, encouraged by Libya's neighbour Egypt, required the government to acknowledge its sympathy for pro-Arab goals by asserting its independence from Western influence. Far from Libya's foreign policy changing because the discovery of oil *allows* it to, foreign policy is changing because popular unrest resulting from the discovery of oil forces it to.' Charles O. Cecil, 'The Determinants of Libyan Foreign Policy,' *Middle East Journal*, Winter, 1965, pp. 27–8.

prestige of the state in its relations with other states and territories within the region automatically facilitates its business with the major powers. Where the great powers, over and above considerations of grand political strategy, have specific commercial and military interests, the techniques of indirect conflict can be very effective. At the time of writing it is still impossible to conceive of an easing of Britain's position in Aden without the good will of Cairo.

But even in an area where a great power, by virtue of long established prescriptive right, can operate without serious fear of interference by other states of its own class, the small power in conflict with it can employ the indirect methods of subversion to strengthen its hand. Thus Cuba in Latin America.[1] Cuba's notable target has been Venezuela[2] and has taken the form of political and material support for the FALN terrorist organization—strikingly so in the last year of President Betancourt's administration (1963). A committee of the Organization of American States has charged Cuba with all the elements of a typical pattern of violent subversion: a systematic propaganda campaign against the Venezuelan Government and incitement to subvert it, training of Venezuelan activists in Cuba for such activities, remittance of funds and supply of arms.[3] It is evident that were the FALN to succeed and take over the country, Cuba's international position within Latin America and with respect to the United States would be revolutionized. But setting such visions to one side, as the Cuban leaders in fact do,[4] much can be achieved in the meantime. With great economy of means the number of points of

[1] Cuban efforts to promote social revolution in Latin America do not appear to have had the backing of the Soviet Union, almost certainly not since the missile crisis of 1962. For all practical purposes it has been acting on its own initiative and on the basis of its own resources.

[2] But also Peru and Colombia. See *United States News and World Report*, 18 October 1965.

[3] Findings quoted in Secretary of State Dean Rusk's address to OAS Foreign Ministers, Washington, 22 July 1964. Also, *The Times*, 20 July 1964.

[4] *The Times*, 30 November 1963.

friction and disturbance are increased and the difficulties of the United States in its attempt to isolate Cuba and marshal the opposition to it throughout Latin America are multiplied. The Cuban problem, seen from Washington, becomes bigger, not smaller. The practical alternatives before the Americans tend to polarize: Cuba must either be crushed or else an accommodation with it sought. So too, in altered form, throughout Latin America. Each régime which sees itself threatened by subversion centred on or sustained by Cuba faces much the same issues: the mere establishment of a *cordon sanitaire* is shown to be not merely useless, but dangerous. Failure to find an accommodation with Havana may lead to loss of power within the home state, or at least to serious internal revolt. But since the Castro Government has demonstrated its relative invulnerability to attempts to employ the same subversive means against it, only the full and overt exercise of national power—and of the United States in particular—is likely to succeed. And such means—blockade, invasion and the like—are ruled out for the present by considerations rooted in inter-American and inter-bloc relations. The Cuban tactic is therefore a broader, political version of one of the now classic principles of guerrilla warfare:

The enemy wanted to concentrate their forces. We compelled them to disperse. By successively launching strong offensives on the points they had left relatively unprotected, we obliged them to scatter their troops all over the place in order to ward off our blows.[1]

It is a daring policy and its ultimate consequences may be disastrous. However, the Cuban leaders seem duly conscious that they are playing for high stakes. This is reflected in Dr. Castro's melodramatic, but fundamentally shrewd comment on the prospect (which he accepts) that the United States

---

[1] Vo Nguyen Giap, op. cit., p. 25. And again: 'We used to say: guerilla (sic) warfare must multiply. To keep itself in life and develop, guerilla warfare has necessarily to develop into mobile warfare. This is a general law.' Ibid., p. 107.

will intervene in Venezuela rather than see the present régime fall:

> If the United States wages war in Venezuela, then brigades of Venezuelans will be formed and sent to the United States—suicide brigades that will show the United States what Venezuelan patriots can do.[1]

IV

The use of subversion as an instrument of state policy is by no means a peculiarity of small states. Until the post war years it was almost exclusively the province of the greater powers, notably Germany and Russia. German subversion under the Nazis—particularly in Austria and the Sudetenland and later in Switzerland—was in many ways akin to what is practiced today in the non-industrial world. But since the war the efforts of the great powers—where the instrument has been employed by them—have been directed towards a different aim: not the aggrandizement of the home base of power so much as the extension or retention of influence on the periphery of power. As a consequence, and not unnaturally, these efforts have often been intermittent, crude and unsuccessful. But they have suffered from a deeper defect. The vitally important communal and other local affinities which offer a kind of moral cover for political co-operation between the dissidents of one state and the government of its neighbour do not apply to the great power which enters this field. Dissidents who seek the aid of great states are either more easily denounceable as traitors and consequently far more vulnerable to detection and punishment, or else entirely cold-blooded and deceitful in their relations with their would-be masters. Either way, the

---

[1] *The Times*, 30 November 1963. In similar vein, President Nasser has explained that:

> Egypt's help to the Aden nationalists had begun as a counter to British support for the Royalists in Yemen, despite his [Nasser's] offer of a 'hand's-off' agreement covering both South Arabia and Yemen. 'From the very beginning,' he said, 'I was in contact with the British Government with Lord Home [who was then Foreign Secretary]. I said: "If you don't interfere in Yemen we shan't interfere in Aden and South Arabia."' (*Observer*, 5 February 1967.)

security of the operation is in constant jeopardy and the net political results doubtful.[1] In contrast the small power which seeks to employ this weapon has the combined benefits of local knowledge and instinctive concentration at the highest level of government on the project in hand and, as a rule, the advantages of one or more categories of affinity between some of its subjects with some of those of its neighbours.

However, the small state is subject to two limitations already alluded to. It can overreach itself and provoke great power intervention—as occurred in Lebanon and Jordan in 1958 and may occur, at some future time, in Latin America. Secondly, it must itself be internally strong. It must be relatively immune to subversion based on other states and be led by men with the necessary degree of ambition and unscrupulousness. It is the latter quality, particularly, which is rare and the combination of a strong state and a weak and vulnerable invironment is rarer still. It is only to be found in the under-developed world. In the firm, stable environment of contemporary north-western Europe such activities are ruled out on both counts. Megalomania and ruthlessness are, mercifully, lacking; and the soft targets on which they would be brought to bear are too. This has the curious, but entirely logical result of permitting states which are undeniably weak by straightforward demographic, military and economic standards to play a far more important and influential international role than inherently stronger and wealthier, but conservative states.

The radical, aggressive states are therefore few in number and there can be no saying how long the international conditions which provide them with so broad a field of manœuvre (by inhibiting the great powers from exercising their influence to the full) will last. The great majority of states which are devoid of assured great power protection

[1] As with, e.g., Soviet activities in Guinea under Ambassador Solod in 1961 and American interference in Syrian affairs in the summer of 1957. For the latter case see Patrick Seale, *The Struggle for Syria*, 1965, pp. 293–5.

have neither the will nor the potentialities to adopt a deliberately active national policy founded on such attempts to
exploit the political and material resources of other states in
the interests of their own. For them the fundamental posture
is *defensive*. It now remains to be seen what such a posture
involves if it is not to be mere acquiescence in the will of
others.

8

THE DEFENSIVE STRATEGY

I

THE national policy of the small power which lacks the impulsion to attempt to increase its total resources at the expense of its neighburs or whose external environment is such that no attempt to do so would succeed must be, in all essential respects, *defensive*. Its relations with the great powers (which are of greatest importance and to which, for convenience, the present discussion will be limited) are characterized, as has been abundantly shown, by a fundamental and growing assymetry of both material and political resources. So long as it is, for all practical diplomatic and military purposes, *alone* in the international arena, the condition of the small state is therefore grounded on a relatively high probability of defeat in any conflict into which it may be drawn and on the ineluctability of defeat where conflict is pursued without restraint. The logic of its relations with the great powers (or with any combination of minor states of equivalent political and military strength) is that national policy must be concerned, in essence with the central questions of how to avoid, mitigate or postpone conflict, and how to resist superior force once conflict has developed.

Coercive pressure, as has been noted, may be of two broad kinds. It may be designed to divide the national leadership, or to loosen its public authority, or to incite opposition— all with the purpose of confronting the effective rulers of the state with a choice between succumbing to the will of the external opponent, on the one hand, and losing their internal authority within the state (along with all the material and immaterial advantages of public office) on the other. Alternatively, it may be designed to attack the state and the society as such. Even the deliberate and total destruction of the social and political fabric of the target state may be envisaged—as by the Germans in Poland in 1939. But whatever the intention, it is clear that a government which commands the support—or at least the obedience—of the overwhelming bulk of the population will be better placed to resist than one which does not. Internal strength narrows the opponent's choice of strategy, compelling him either to adopt harsher measures than he might otherwise wish to employ, or to abandon or at least greatly modify his basic policy. In other words, the internal strength of a régime is its first line of defence in the face of external pressure or attack. Where the attack is generalized and unrestrained—as in Poland— aggression may actually increase national cohesion and loyalty to the government—since the population will, in fact, be offered no material alternative. But such cases apart, external pressure is likely to corrode internal strength and the greater the pressure the greater must be the internal stability and cohesion of the society under attack at the outset of conflict if resistance is to be maintained for any period thereafter. A very deeply entrenched régime will, in principle, have the option of bringing the whole edifice of state crashing down upon it, rather than accept dictation from abroad; and if its opponents credit it with the will and the capacity to do so, i.e. to resist regardless of consequences, its political position will be improved. But the basic disparity in material strength will not be affected thereby and the material consequences of conflict as such will not be mitigated by the determination with which they are met. The diplomatic advantages of obduracy follow from the consequential narrowing of the opponent's choice of weapons. They fade, however, once the firing (or economic pressure) begins in earnest.

The incurable disparity of strength between the small state and its major opponents might appear to be less pronounced where and when international relations are founded upon, and by consent largely limited to, milder forms of influence—traditional diplomacy, attempts to manipulate public opinion, and other, similar appeals to the intellect and the emotions rather than to fear of dire material consequences. But the most cursory review of events since the beginning of the present century would surely indicate that their efficacy is limited in the extreme. Traditional, persuasive diplomacy and the related arts of propaganda and lobbying may be employed to some purpose, even by a small power, but only provided the national interest of the target country is either undefined with respect to the issue in question, or uncertain, or subject to serious internal debate. Where, on the contrary, it is clear and present in the minds of the makers of policy even the firmest treaty obligations lose their sanctity, as the Czechoslovak Government discovered in September 1938, let alone the much more tenuous obligations inherent in general international law and custom. Nor is there anything in the experience of either the League of Nations or the United Nations Organization to suggest otherwise. Only states which have no clear, definable interest in the issue in question (e.g. the Latin American States on the various Middle Eastern conflicts) are prepared to adopt even a verbal position which is in any significant sense unaffected by considerations of national policy. Where states are involved in the particular conflict, and, *ex hypothesi*, have an interest in its resolution in one manner rather than another, a purely legal or moral appeal to the principles and provisions of the United Nations Charter, for example, will be without effect or simply be countered dialectically, as much for form's sake as for any other purpose. Nor is it unknown for small states in conflict with others and without friends at court to be refused even formal recourse to the United Nations. Thus the United States managed to force an impending discussion of its conflict with Guatemala in June 1954, out of the Security Council and into the Organization of American States where it was better placed to handle it;[1] and more recently, the request of the Rhodesian Government (whose *de facto* authority was never in doubt) to be heard by the Council when sanctions against it were debated in December 1966, was carefully ignored, despite clear provisions in the Charter making such an appearance possible.[2] None of this detracts from the importance of the UN as a forum for the airing and—on occasion—resolution of conflict. Nor from its particular function as a veil behind which states which have over-committed and over-reached themselves can afford to retreat from exposed political and military positions on such formal, face-saving grounds as that they are acting in support of, and out of loyalty to, the Organization rather than as a consequence of error and defeat. The contribution of the United Nations to international security in aggregate is a real one; but in particular cases no country can afford to rely upon it for succour unless there are other member states of sufficient power and influence to rally behind it to good effect—and then, of course, it will be their power and influence that will be expected to decide the issue, not membership in, or formal recourse to, the Organization.

International law in the strictest sense and as handed down in the judgments of the International Court of Justice at The Hague is in a different case. There are certainly some precedents for the hard-pressed, but politically isolated state being granted a favourable decision where there is formal warrant for it. But few political issues of importance are amenable to legal treatment and still fewer are the instances

---

[1] Guatemala had appealed to the Security Council to induce Honduras and Nicaragua to 'secure the cessation of all assistance to the [U.S.-backed] mercenary forces which are continuing to invade the national territory of Guatemala.' On 25 June the Security Council, in what was formally a procedural vote not to include the subject in its agenda, resolved to postpone further discussion pending a report from an OAS fact-finding mission. By the time the mission arrived in Guatemala on 29 June President Arbenz had resigned and a cease-fire was being negotiated between a new *junta* and the insurgents. In the Security Council only Brazil, Colombia, Nationalist China and Turkey had supported the United States; the Soviet Union, Lebanon and New Zealand had opposed it, while Britain and France had abstained.

[2] Article 32.

of both sides to a serious political conflict being prepared to submit to adjudication in good faith and with the genuine intention of abiding by an unfavourable judgement, if need be. In any case, the execution of a judgment of the International Court in the face of a default devolves upon the Security Council, and in the affairs of the Council it is the *political* component of international problems that is, and by design, decisive. In the language of the Charter '. . . the Security Council . . . may, if it deems necessary, make recommendations or decide upon measures to be taken to give effect to the judgment.'[1] Neither the great power veto in the Council, nor, of course, the political considerations of the individual members in the light of which every matter of substance before the United Nations is finally decided, can be circumvented by recourse to international justice.

Of more importance for the isolated state is the variety of limited, contingent levers of influence that small states, as well as large, may find themselves blessed with. These are chiefly functions of geographical circumstances such as location in, or proximity to, areas of conflict and strategic importance and possession of rare or valued natural resources. There may also be such ephemeral political advantages as occur when the vote at the United Nations is particularly close or when the presence or co-operation of certain states on international bodies is thought desirable— to cite two of a myriad of minor possibilities. But such advantages, however real and useful, can rarely be deliberate creations of national policy and are only barely amenable to political manipulation. They are windfall profits and as such not to be relied on for more than a very limited period. A change in the international weather, a leap forward in civil and military technological development, and they are instantly reduced in value. Moreover, they can be exploited, if at all, only by negative means, by threatened or actual refusal of facilities, trade or political co-operation. And thus, far from mitigating conflict, the exploitation of such advantages

[1] Article 94, section 2.

tends to exacerbate it. In many cases, moreover, the direct economic costs for the small state of such an attempt to employ the weapon of deprivation may be very high, weakening the state materially when it has greatest reason to garner all its strength. So broadly speaking, where a small state is in possession of a strategic or commercial or political facility which is required by a greater state, the facility can only be exploited to advantage in relation to relatively minor issues and then only provided it is not too highly prized by the opponent. Once the threat to withhold it becomes real enough to perturb the major power the facility is itself converted into a subject of conflict and the greater the value or importance attached to it the more severe the conflict that develops subsequently is likely to be. Alternatively, it is dispensed with by the greater power and any benefit that might have been drawn from it is lost. In short, the use of such contingent geographical and political advantages is only a little less limited in scope than the employment of purely political and diplomatic instruments of state and the consequences of too heavy a reliance upon them may be disastrous. Whatever tactical benefit may be derived from them is likely, on the balance, to be outweighed by the long-term consequences of constituting an obvious strategic or commercial prize for any major state sufficiently powerful or self-confident to attempt to seize it. In this sense it is a moot point whether Turkey's possession of the Straits, or Iran's oil or the Panamanian and Egyptian Canals can rightly be judged advantages at all, if the revenue element is excluded from consideration. At all events, it is clear that in the event of over-playing such a hand and as a pre-condition of any attempt to exploit it successfully, or even simply being free to govern its passive use, a substantial military capability to defend it is indispensable. The canny way in which the Swiss military leadership managed to exploit their position athwart the main lines of communication between the Axis powers during the Second World War—wherein lay both their strength and their weakness—was founded, in the last resort, on the effectiveness of the Swiss defence forces and the plan for a defendable *reduit national.*

The twin problems of how to avoid, mitigate or postpone conflict with a superior power on the one hand, and how to resist superior force on the other, must therefore be considered in the light of what is likely to be the national interest of the superior power in any concrete case. The capacity of the small state to avoid, soften or resist conflict will depend upon the extent to which it can create a contradiction, *for its opponent,* between the *prima facie* advantages of pursuing the conflict to the end and the advantages of some alternative course. In the political sphere this means, in effect, a capacity to create or encourage an interest that is common to both states. In the military sphere this means the ability to deter.

II

An interest that is common to two states can be of two kinds. It can relate principally to matters which concern the welfare of the two states in question and be dealt with in a bilateral framework which largely excludes questions of wider, international relevance. Economic and cultural affairs, communications, scientific and technological development and the other bread and butter subjects of inter-state relations are of this category. But because of the absolute limits of the small state's economic and social resources, the political value of such co-operation can never be great. Alternatively, a common interest can relate to general international problems involving conflict with, or influence over, third parties and which pose questions of the policy to be adopted towards them. An element of understanding, usually secret, and of commitment which may be secret initially, but which must be revealed ultimately in behaviour are implied. The dividing line between the two classes of co-operation is rarely entirely clear and it would be pedantic to insist that agreement on a given subject of common interest must pertain to one or the other. It may well pertain to both simultaneously. What matters for the

unaligned state is that the latter class implies that a choice
has been taken to support another state in a matter which
concerns a third party which has not been privy to the understanding and to which no commitments have been made.

In formal terms this is a limited negation of non-
alignment. The practical consequences are more important.
A bilateral political understanding—so long as the general
condition of non-alignment is maintained—can only be *ad
hoc* and the commitments entered into can only be of restricted scope and duration. Long-term evolution of
political and strategic needs cannot be catered for within
such a scheme. The political price paid by the two parties—
the great and the small—is therefore unequal. The great
power acquires a temporary advantage for which it pays a
limited price, but it is not required to undertake the burden
of a long-term commitment to another state. Its own general,
international situation remains unchanged. The unaligned
state, by entering into a short-term political understanding
relating to a third state automatically weakens the principal
political advantage of its situation, namely, that by remaining
uncommitted to the parties in any given conflict it adds
nothing to the strength of either side. Non-alignment is
very far from constituting a guarantee of the security of any
state, but such value as it has is dependent on the confidence
of all sides that it will be maintained throughout the foreseeable future. Any deviation from neutrality (in the strictly
political, non-legal sense of the term) registers as a possible
omen of, or precedent for, further deviations. The benefits
of non-alignment, however small, will thus be eroded and the
penalties for deviation added to the fundamental weakness
of the condition itself. Thus political co-operation with respect to third parties only makes sense as a prelude to entry
into firm and binding commitments, i.e. an abandonment of
non-alignment, or else when conflict with the other side is
viewed as unavoidable. Where no firm commitments can be
hoped for from the major partner, but where for economic
and other reasons such deviations from non-alignment are

forced upon the state, or deemed an unavoidable price to pay for trade and strategic facilities, the ultimate penalties may be heavy. Thus, even apart from the objective limits to the small state's capacity to create, or be party to, a common purpose with a major power, such benefits as it may derive from political co-operation can only be short-term, while the harm done to its general international situation may be irreparable. Above all, as a method of staving off or mitigating conflict political co-operation with a major power is in the long run self-defeating. The political resources of the state, such as they are, are weakened and difficulties with one side are only softened at the cost of difficulties with the other. Unless exercised with much self-denying caution political co-operation degenerates into Danegeld.

The validity of such a model of the consequences of political co-operation with a major power is clearly greatest in a bi-polar world. For in a structure of international relations dominated by two great powers the condition of non-alignment is doubly difficult. Conflict between the two centres makes the exercise of any political choice by third parties signify a measure of identification with one side—without necessarily any compensating protection by either. On the other hand, accommodation between the world centres leaves no room for choice whatsoever. Only the 'suicidal alternative' remains. But the greater the number of effective centres of power and, particularly, of supply of economic and strategic essentials, the less likely is the small state to be faced with stark alternatives and the less distinct are the political implications and the softer are the consequences of *ad hoc* political co-operation with any single one. The value of the small state's amity and of any contingent advantages it may possess are similarly enhanced. The third, fourth and fifth centres of world power stand in greater need of both the material and political benefits of association with minor states. And while none of this may save the minor state or protect it from conflict with any one of the world powers, the complexity of its relationships and joint interests with other major states may serve to mitigate that conflict in some measure. It is, more than anything, the uncertainty and lack of clear and permanent focus in international affairs implied by a multi-centred world with its crossed lines of influence and many-sided issues that ease the situation of the small power. But for full advantage to be taken of the uncertainties the condition of non-alignment, itself one of uncertainty and lack of clear, positive commitment and definition, is indispensable. Here, the logic of non-alignment is a double one: a multi-centred world is required to reduce the consequences of dependence uncompensated by protection; and, at the same time, without a group of unaligned states serving, as it were, as an international floating vote, the prospect of new and effective centres of world power are limited. Prince Norodom Sihanouk of Cambodia has put it well:

Si je vais à Paris, c'est surtout pour remercier les Français de ce qu'ils ont fait pour le Cambodge, et surtout au cours des dernières années. Sans la France, sans sa politique intelligente, les déceptions dont nous ont abreuvés les Américains, et même les Anglais—dont les traditions de réalisme semblent se perdre—nous auraient profondément détournés de l'Occident. C'est la France qui a jeté et maintenu un pont entre le monde libre et nous. C'est grâce à la France que le Cambodge n'a pas basculé dans le camp socialiste et peut toujours se dire neutre . . . Vous savez, je critique beaucoup l'OTASE, et la présence américaine à Bangkok. Mais, à franchement parler, autant je suis hostile à la présence de l'US Army au Vietnam, où elle ne sert qu'à fabriquer des communistes, autant je suis favorable à son maintien en Thailande. Je me sens plus solide ainsi, plus . . . neutre.[1]

III

The capacity of a small state to deter a major power from using military force against it cannot be usefully discussed in absolute terms. There can be no deterrent in the full sense that the potential aggressor has to weigh the consequences of defeat or even, more simply, the inability to achieve vic-

---

[1] *Le Monde*, 24 June 1964. See also Bernard K. Gordon, 'Cambodia: Where Foreign Policy Counts', *Asian Survey*, September 1965.

tory in the field. A relation comparable to that which may obtain between two world powers cannot occur. Deterrence by a small power means something substantially more limited based on two essential, *a priori* assumptions. The first is that no small state can, in itself, constitute a major target of great power policy, but only one which is secondary to a more important object. The second is that if the price of exercising military pressure against it can be raised high enough, other, less costly means of achieving the major object will be preferred. Such have been the strategic assumptions underlying Swedish defence policy for many years. In a television interview in 1964 the Swedish Prime Minister was asked:

Sweden's front-line is the Baltic coast. Sweden stands without allies in the event of attack. How long does Sweden think she can hold out against an aggressor and where does she expect any possible help to come from?

Prime Minister Erlander replied that:

I do not believe that Sweden could be an objective to be attacked except in conjunction with a major conflict. There is no reason for an isolated attack on Sweden and we do not therefore take such an attack much into account.

In a major conflict, as experience has gone to show, even the Great Powers must plan the use of their resources, large though they are, and they cannot afford to throw in overwhelming troop concentrations against a minor secondary objective. Accordingly we are building up a defence which has naturally not much of a chance of surviving against a concentrated attack by a Great Power but which, nevertheless, may be rather troublesome to overcome if Sweden is a secondary objective. We have pursued this policy during the last two world wars and I believe that Sweden's present defence fulfils the same function, that is to say, to see that Sweden is not easily conquered and does not become a military vacuum. This is why we have chosen to build up our defence in this way, a defence which I believe to be rather strong as you gentlemen may have had an opportunity of seeing. We know that our Air Force is one of the strongest in the world and that it is in a position to put its resources rapidly into action.[1]

[1] Royal Ministry of Foreign Affairs, *Documents on Swedish Foreign Policy, 1964,* Stockholm, 1965, p. 30.

Similarly, the doctrine underlying the current Swiss defence effort, according to an authoritative spokesman, is not simply to provide combat units which will hit back at an invader in deference to the principle that the national territory must be defended, but 'to deliver such crippling blows, inflicting such heavy casualties, and shake his morale to such a degree that he may decide to abandon his purpose'.[1]

This, in turn, is in the tradition of General Guisan's strategy for Switzerland during the Second World War which was founded on the belief that a direct German attack could be avoided if the German High Command knew it would lead to a prolonged and costly campaign, creating a new battlefield in Central Europe and serious disruption to existing plans.[2]

It follows, however, that where the attainment of the major target is clearly conditional upon attainment of the minor target such a deterrent collapses—unless it is so successful that it leads the potential aggressor to reassess his broad strategy entirely. Thus the disagreement between Hitler and his generals over the timing and details of Operation Green—the plan for the invasion of Czechoslovakia on 1 October 1938 which the Munich Agreement forestalled—was, in some respects, a disagreement not only over the correct evaluation of the Czech defences and the Germans' capacity to overcome them, but over the conquest of Czechoslovakia *per se*. For the generals the major objects of German policy lay elsewhere and they disliked Operation Green not only because it was risky, but because there seemed to them insufficient justification for executing it at that particular stage of the rearmament and reorganization of the German armed forces. For Hitler, in contrast, Czechoslovakia was then a major object of policy and its destruction was an essential preliminary, in his view, to

[1] A Swiss Army corps commander to the *Neue Züricher Zeitung* quoted in the *Guardian*, 14 July 1960.

[2] Cf. General Guisan's Memorandum of 12 July 1940, in André Guex (Ed.), *Général Guisan*, Lausanne, 1960, pp. 48–49.

further progress. It was therefore useless for the generals to argue that the Czech defences were strong and their capacity to break through them uncertain. However, had the Czechs been weaker militarily the debate between Hitler and his generals would never have occurred in the first place.[1] And had the Czechs stood fast and succeeded, as their Chief of Staff hoped, in stopping the advance of the Germans in its initial stages in some sectors, if not all, it is reasonable to suppose that the debate between Hitler and his principal generals would have started up anew. It is not simply the symbolic value of an armed defensive capability that matters, or the ability to put up any kind of defence, no matter how limited. It is the absolute strength that is decisive —here as in most cases of military confrontation.

The difficulty today, as has been shown, is that for economic and technological reasons it has become increasingly difficult for the small state to stay the course, even excluding the questions raised by the great powers' possession of nuclear weapons.[2] If Sweden today, and to a lesser extent Switzerland too, have been able to maintain a defence establishment of sufficient quality and size to provide them with a credible *conventional* deterrent capability in the postwar period in the limited sense of the term used here, it seems less certain that they will be able to do so in the future. It seems even more unlikely that, say, a

---

[1] The forces mobilized by the Czechs on 23 September 1938, were roughly equal in number and armaments to the German forces scheduled to go into action seven days later.

[2] See next chapter. The justification for giving any measure of serious consideration to a small power's conventional military power where its potential opponent possesses nuclear weapons is two-fold. Firstly, Korea, Hungary, Suez and Vietnam were all scenes of conflict between great and small powers, but in no case were non-conventional arms employed. It is extremely difficult to envisage fresh conflicts of this order whose severity will be so much greater and to which so much more importance will be attached that the use of nuclear weapons by the major side will be thought necessary. Secondly, the employment of nuclear weapons in itself would automatically convert even the most limited, regional conflict into one of profound importance to all the powers. It could thus evolve into a different kind of war and its strategic circumstances would duly change. However, if the minor power were to possess nuclear weapons too the first point would no longer apply and the second would have different implications, as will be argued in the chapter that follows.

neutralized Thailand can be in a position to deter China militarily now or at any time, or Finland the Soviet Union. The discrepancy in conventional, let alone unconventional power between minor and major states is growing; and if, in 1938, it took the megalomania of Hitler to overcome the professional resistance of his generals to Operation Green, it may be thought that in the distant, but still foreseeable future, and given equivalent circumstances, such strong professional objections are unlikely to recur.

None of this means that the small, unaligned states are irrevocably due for liquidation and that the pattern set by the Germans in Austria and Czechoslovakia in 1938–9 will necessarily be repeated in our times until only a few vast empires or power blocs remain to confront each other in a much simplified world. Speculation need not be carried that far. The rising difficulties of maintaining a deterrent capability do mean, however, that the last autonomous basis of the independence of the small states is in process of erosion and that the unequal and assymetrical relations between them and certain major states are solidifying. For the future, Finland may be the paradigm of the small, independent state, not Sweden.

The formal sovereignty of Finland is not in question, but its independence of action and freedom of choice are subject to limits set by the Soviets, generally understood by the Finns and tacitly accepted by the other powers both in and beyond Scandinavia. At the heart of Finnish foreign policy is the intention to give the Russians no cause to doubt the Finns' determination to remain outside military alliances and to maintain friendly relations with the Soviet Union. The Finnish military effort, restricted in any case by treaty obligations, is of lower priority and import. As a consequence the Finns have had to reject the offer to participate in the Marshall Plan, to seek Russian agreement to their associa- tion with EFTA, to have believed it wiser to turn down an opportunity of membership in the Security Council and to have suffered a substantial degree of interference in their domestic affairs (towards the end of 1958).[1] Finally, it is inconceivable today, unlike 1939, that the western powers consider intervention in case of renewed conflict between Russia and a rebellious Finland.

This long and complex process by which the relative power of small states seems likely to be reduced beyond the point at which they can hope to deter great powers to any effective degree is one that has been long in the making and may not end for many years, perhaps for several decades. Many such states are already affected. Others are not due to suffer the consequences for some time. For the latter group two questions may arise and appear to require careful answers.

The first question that policy-makers may have to ask themselves is how much value they ought to continue to attach to the retention of a defensive, military option, considering the great social and economic effort it entails and as contrasted with the slender underpinning for national security it provides even in the best of circumstances. Dependence on the goodwill of strangers is commonly disagreeable to thinking men, but sensitivity on this score may lapse in time, even in those neutral European states where it is traditionally very strong. Alternatively, minds may turn increasingly to the search for a political solution: federation with other states similarly placed, alliance with major powers or, more simply, a tacit recognition that in crisis the condition of non-alignment must be abandoned and accommodation sought with a protecting power. Of that there are some signs already, notably in Switzerland[2] and Sweden.[3] But to

---

[1] Cf. Kalevi J. Holsti, 'Strategy and techniques of influence in Soviet–Finnish relations', *Western Political Quarterly*, March 1964; and John H. Wuorinen, 'Finland and the USSR—1945–61', *Journal of International Affairs*, 1962, xvi, No. 1.

[2] Cf. Elizabeth Wiskemann, 'The state of Switzerland in 1956', *International Affairs*, October 1956, pp. 437–8; *Sunday Telegraph*, 12 February 1961, p. 28; and Brigadier W. F. K. Thompson, 'Switzerland may have second thoughts', *Daily Telegraph*, 10 October 1961.

[3] Cf. Herbert Tingsten, 'Issues in Swedish Foreign Policy', *Foreign Affairs*, April 1959, pp. 478–9.

be effective, such political solutions, whether clear and public, or informal, or even secret, must be devised and accepted in advance of a crisis. In other words, the great decisions must be taken before the state, in principle at least, is in need of them. They are correspondingly difficult to take. Nor do all small, politically solitary states have the option of emerging from isolation at will.

It seems therefore that a second question is bound to arise in the course of the formulation or reformulation of national policy—and which in some cases has already arisen and been keenly debated. It is the question whether the period in which the military establishment can be maintained on a sufficiently high quantitative and qualitative level to give grounds for confidence that it will fulfil its limited deterrent function cannot be significantly extended by a radical change in the character of the weapons on which it is based, i.e. by the adoption of nuclear arms.

9

THE NUCLEAR WEAPONS FACTOR

I

THE question of nuclear power puts into the sharpest possible focus the central dilemma of the small unaligned state: insistence on the pursuit of what, on one level, appears to be the national interest, even within the limits of an essentially defensive policy, may lead, on another level and when faced with major opposition, to defeat, even to self-destruction. In an important respect the difference between a major and a minor state lies in the evident fact that, given careful, rational and unremitting attention to its political, military and economic defences the great state is immune to all but cataclysmic attack and that, even in such an event, it remains within its power to wreak enormous havoc on its enemies. The minor state is not only unable to wreak such havoc, it is vulnerable to pressure and attack of a quite different—because vastly reduced—order. Above all, there may be circumstances where it may even be unable to engage in the strengthening of its defensive dispositions without courting greater, often self-defeating, dangers—greater, in fact, than its strengthened defences were designed and could be designed to meet. The obvious quantitative differences between the major and the minor states are thus converted into no less important qualitative distinctions of which the small power must be continually aware if it is not to overstep the narrow boundaries of its autonomous strength. Failure to resist marginal encroachment on its political independence, failure to maintain its defences and failure to put its resources to maximum use make it correspondingly more vulnerable to political, military and economic pressure. Failure to resist such pressure seals the small state's political fate and converts independence, however fragile and limited, into vassalage, however sweetened by respect for the forms of sovereignty. But resistance to pressure when it *is* exerted in full by one or more major powers is liable to lead to disaster. In consequence, so long as value is attached to political independence—and, as has been suggested, there are societies where this is no longer the case, even in the contemporary period—the heart of the problem of non-alignment is how to avoid conflict and deter the mightier opponent from putting the state's civil and military defences to the test.

The effectiveness of the small state's capacity for passive (economic) and active (military) resistance varies, of course, with the character and elements of the broader political and military circumstances in which the conflict is placed. The wise statesman of the small power is thus impelled to plan for the most difficult, least helpful of contingencies. For the same reason, the great powers, even where they do not anticipate conflict, cannot regard a substantial increment of strength which accrues to a small power with particular favour, or only in very special circumstances. The stronger the small states' capacity to resist and maintain an independent political course and the greater the damage they can inflict on their enemies in the event of attack, the more restricted are the great powers in their own political and military movements. For this reason, if for no other, the prospect of the acquisition of nuclear weapons by minor states leading, ostensibly, to a dramatic change in the pattern of military power is a source of considerable alarm:

When we consider the costs to us of trying to stop the spread of nuclear weapons, we should not lose sight of the fact that widespread nuclear proliferation would mean a substantial erosion in the margin of power which our great wealth and industrial base have long given us relative to much of the rest of the world.

Thus an authoritative American spokesman.[1] The Russians

---

[1] William C. Foster (Director, United States Arms Control and Disarmament Agency), 'New Directions in Arms Control and Disarmament', *Foreign Affairs*, July 1965, p. 591.

have been less candid, but have certainly not disguised their hostility to the acquisition of such weapons by other countries. The Chinese view is unclear. Their formal position is that they themselves developed nuclear weapons in order to break the 'nuclear monopoly', that they will never be the first to use them, and that they want complete prohibition and destruction of existing weapons. They have said little about the general problem of nuclear proliferation, but the logic of their position is that if some powers possess nuclear weapons other powers cannot be denied the right to develop them.[1] However, it may be plausibly argued that even their view is conditional on their own continued isolation and that, moreover, it would in all probability change if small and hostile nations on China's periphery were to show evidence of effective candidacy for the 'club'. Under the cloud of conscious and unconscious humbug[2] which often obscures the undeniably grave and fateful problem of nuclear proliferation deep concern lest the great powers lose their ultimate control over events as the military sanctions on which it rests become available to others may be discerned.

[1] No other construction can be put on the following passage in Chou En-lai's message to the 11th World Conference Against A- and H-Bombs in Tokyo, July 1965:

United States imperialism has conducted hundreds of nuclear tests and manufactured and stockpiled large quantities of nuclear weapons. Its nuclear bases, nuclear submarines and nuclear-capable planes are stationed all over the world. In these circumstances, does not the so-called banning of nuclear tests and prevention of nuclear proliferation actually give the United States the prerogative to maintain its nuclear monopoly and practise nuclear blackmail for purposes of aggression, while depriving other countries of their right to develop nuclear weapons and resist the U.S. nuclear threat in self-defence? (*Peking Review*, 30 July 1965, p. 4.)

[2] E.g. Senator Robert Kennedy: '. . . prevention of nuclear spread is a matter of political action on a grand scale—an effort to turn the world community away from nuclear war, away from ultimate weapons as guarantors of security and prestige.' (*Congressional Record-Senate*, 13 October 1965, p. 25890.) Since there is no evidence that Senator Kennedy wishes the United States to move away from 'ultimate weapons' on which its own 'security and prestige' rest so firmly, his passionate pleas for an end to nuclear proliferation must be seen as founded on much the same fears as the more candid view put forward by Mr. Foster. The sincerity of his feelings are not in doubt, but his language perfectly exemplifies that optical distortion that affects the leaders of great powers when they come to consider the affairs of minor states.

The probability that minor states actually acquire nuclear weapons is a subject which has been examined in great detail in recent years;[1] but three points may be noted. The first is that there are a number of states in the class of small powers that have shown—or been thought by competent observers to have shown[2]—an active interest in the subject. Secondly, given the will to produce such weapons and the readiness to accept the political and military difficulties that would probably ensue, it is clearly no longer beyond the economic strength of a small, industrialized state to support the contingent costs and it may even be within the economic bounds of a semi-industrialized state (such as Egypt). Colonel W. Mark of the Swiss Army suggested some years ago that at a cost of an additional 10 per cent. of the normal military budget, or 0·3 per cent. of the Gross National Product, Switzerland could undertake a programme leading to the production of the first (fission) warhead after ten years of research and development. Over a further decade between 30 and 40 warheads could be produced.[3] Acceptance of a higher rate of annual cost would speed up the programme. A more recent, but more generalized calculation has suggested that a limited nuclear capability of the type maintained and being developed by Britain and France would require an average additional expenditure of some $300 million over ten years. This would increase annual defence expenditure (as a percentage of GNP) for certain states as follows: Sweden—by 1·7 per cent.; Switzerland—by 1·8 per cent.; Belgium—by 1·8 per cent.; Netherlands—by 1·8 per cent.; and Czechoslovakia—by 1·6 per

---

[1] See in particular: Leonard Beaton and John Maddox, *The Spread of Nuclear Weapons*, 1962; Leonard Beaton, *Must the Bomb Spread?*, 1966; R. N. Rosecrance (Ed.), *The Dispersion of Nuclear Weapons*, New York, 1964; Alastair Buchan (Ed.), *A World of Nuclear Powers?*, Englewood Cliffs, N.J., 1966.

[2] Beaton and Maddox, op. cit.; Beaton, op. cit.; *Newsweek*, 9 August 1965; and *Survival*, September–October, 1963, p. 195. Those mentioned include: Australia, Belgium, Czechoslovakia, East Germany, Israel, the Netherlands, South Africa, Sweden, Switzerland and the United Arab Republic (Egypt).

[3] Colonel W. Mark, 'Armes atomiques pour l'armée suisse—Pouvoir ou Vouloir?', *Revue Militaire Suisse*, December 1963.

cent.[1] A calculation of this kind is subject to great variation, particularly on the score of the delivery system being planned for in conjunction with the warheads. But they suggest what order of magnitude is involved. There can be little doubt that on economic grounds, at any rate, a nuclear project can be judged a feasible one. Thirdly, in at least two states—Sweden and Switzerland—there have been reasonably frank and public debates on the military advisability of acquiring nuclear weapons and though neither government has finally committed itself one way or the other, senior military and political figures including a Swedish Commander-in-Chief and a President of the Swiss Confederation (Dr. Wahlen) have expressed themselves in favour.[2]

It is the strategic implications of the acquisition of nuclear power that pose the crucial dilemma for the small state. As a topic it is, of course, doubly speculative. Firstly, like all attempts to envisage nuclear war, actual or impending, argument must rest on a set of technical and psychological assumptions for which the most that can be said is that they are believed to be plausible. Secondly, no small state has yet acquired a nuclear armoury, nor, so far as is known at the time of writing, has one even resolved in principle to do so. And since different states, if they were to make the attempt, would have widely differing ends (and opponents) in view, it is difficult even to speculate on the subject without outlining fairly rigid models which are unlikely to obtain in practice except in very approximate terms.

With these reservations in mind two situations may be usefully distinguished. One is where nuclear weapons are acquired with the purpose of strengthening a defensive policy or posture; the other is where the purpose is the

---

[1] Leonard Beaton, 'Capabilities of Non-Nuclear Powers' in Alastair Buchan, op. cit., p. 36.

[2] There is a substantial literature arising out of the Swedish and Swiss debates on the subject. Two useful summaries of the cases for acquisition are: General Adolph Westring, 'Le problème des armes atomiques en Suède', *Revue Militaire Générale*, March 1958; and U. Aebi and others, 'La Suisse et son équipement en armes atomiques', in Société d'études militaires, *Evolution de l'Armée suisse, Documentation*, Cahier No. 11, 1962.

strengthening of an active or aggressive policy.[1] Each will be considered in turn.

II

The fundamental situation, which is at the same time the one most likely to occur, is where a minor power seeks maximum *deterrent* power through the acquisition of maximum military force. On the face of it, nuclear weapons seem to offer a near-perfect solution to all three of the small state's most acute military problems. The astronomic increase in fire-power which they provide would offset the absolute limits on numbers of fighting personnel and the pieces of military equipment they can conveniently handle. The damage that can be done even a great enemy would be so extensive as to suggest that technological obsolescence would cease to be a principal determinant of the effectiveness of the national military establishment as a credible deterrent. And, lastly, the possession of nuclear arms appear to provide the only possible answer to the question how any state can propose to face a threat from another which is itself armed with such weapons over and above superior conventional forces.

Le moyen le plus efficace jusqu'à présent pour empêcher une guerre est l'arme atomique. Si la Suède disposait d'armes atomiques, cela freinerait plus qu'autre chose un agresseur éventuel, en le forçant à peser le pour et le contre d'une attaque contre la Suède. Son hesitation serait motivée par la perspective de pertes militaires fortement augmentées . . .[2]

Both in Sweden and Switzerland, those who favour the acquisition of nuclear weapons tend to restrict the demand to one for arms suitable for tactical use, which is to say against advancing forces and, possibly, against interdiction targets—railway junctions, bridges, airfields and the like.[3]

---

[1] Cf. Chapters 7 and 8 above.   [2] General Adolph Westring, op. cit.

[3] It is more convenient to talk of tactical *targets* than of tactical *weapons*, if only because it is evident that so-called strategic weapons can in certain cases be employed against tactical targets. However, even the term tactical targets is somewhat misleading, as will be shown below.

In the simplest possible terms the idea is that since the deployment of nuclear arms will induce the enemy to disperse his forces the possibility of a massed invasion spearhead by land or by sea is much reduced and one of the great power's principal advantages—the ability to concentrate overwhelming forces at any single point of the defences—will have been lost. If both sides possess nuclear weapons suitable for use against such tactical targets both will have to avoid the massing of forces, but the side with the most complex and extended logistical support is likely to suffer most. In the present context this would be to the advantage of the defender because he is closer to his base and operating on home ground. The invader would have to make a greater military investment than would otherwise be the case, encounter greater obstacles to his purpose, be forced to operate on a much higher and more complex level of tactics and command *whether or not* nuclear weapons were actually employed: the possession of them by the defender inhibiting procedures that would otherwise be safe to adopt. Furthermore, if the invader is himself prepared to use nuclear weapons he knows that there will be response in kind, while the defending forces will be morally strengthened by the fact that they will not be exposed unilaterally to the unknown horrors of nuclear warfare. The possibilities for blackmail and terror propaganda inherent in a situation where only one side possesses such weapons will thus be substantially reduced. And, lastly, the prospect of nuclear warfare as such may incite other powers to intervene where a conventional invasion or invasion-threat might be passed over in silence.[1]

---

[1] It is not claimed that all Swiss and Swedish military experts who advocate acquisition of nuclear weapons hold this view; it is sufficient that some appear to do so. Nor are experts, generally, agreed about either the advantages or the implications of the tactical use of nuclear weapons. Still less is it the present purpose to argue for or against it. However, unless a summary and necessarily somewhat superficial account of the apparent advantages is given it is impossible, logically, to look more closely at the implications of 'going nuclear' and it is these that are of interest here. In addition to the articles cited, useful discussions of the problem from a variety of points of view are to be found in: General Ailleret, 'Flexible Response: A French View', *Survival*, November–December 1964, reprinted from *Revue de Défense Nationale*, August–September 1964; Neville Brown, *Nuclear War, The Impending*

A closer examination of the question suggests that this relatively simple view of the advantages of the nuclear deterrent is as inadequate as was the doctrine of massive retaliation in the very different circumstances of the Soviet-American conflict in the first fifteen years or so after the Second World War. It relies on the implicit assumption that neither party will employ nuclear weapons 'strategically', in particular against the population centres of the opposing side. But such an assumption rests, in turn, on grounds that differ with the size and strength of the state concerned and thus exposes the fact that the acquisition of nuclear weapons does not automatically 'equalize' small and great nor even, necessarily, reduce the gap between them. Under certain circumstances it may enhance the discrepancies.

The two most important parameters here are the size of the nation (in terms of area and population) and the strength of the nuclear force (in terms of warheads and delivery systems). Where both states are approximately equal at a high level in each respect a strategic deadlock—stable or unstable, however one may wish to see it—may obtain after the manner of the nuclear balance that obtained between the United States and the Soviet Union before the question of anti-missile defence began to be raised. Where the states are unequal such a deadlock is unlikely (quite apart from the question of anti-missile defence), or at all events will have an entirely different character. The main reason for this is that while the damage that the major nuclear power (taking Russia or America as the model) can inflict on the minor one is very nearly total, the minor power, even if it should acquire a counter-city capability, cannot inflict damage that is proportionate to its own strength, let alone total. The

Strategic Deadlock, 1964, pp. 194, 198–200, 210–19; M. E. Geneste and L. M. Jones, 'Professional Views on Tactical Weapons', *Survival*, September–October 1962, reprinted from *Military Review*, July 1962; B. H. Liddell Hart, *Deterrent or Defence*, 1960, p. 79; General Pickert, 'The Value of Numbers in the Nuclear Age', *Survival*, September–October 1961, reprinted from *Revue Militaire Générale*, February 1961.

sophistication and comprehensiveness of the major power's air defences will always be greater than that of the minor power. Should they include an anti-missile capability, to which, on present showing, the small state cannot aspire because of the huge expense that is entailed, the discrepancy will be decisive. Moreover, while the major power will be able to execute a counter-force strike, the minor power cannot, if only because that would imply weapon production on a quantitative scale not much smaller than that of the major powers.

It has been argued, however, notably by General Pierre Gallois,[1] that the deterrent can be proportionate, which is to say that where the strike capacity, however small, of the minor state is more than proportionate to the prize implied by its conquest or defeat the advantages of attacking it will be cancelled out and that, in consequence, it would suffice for a small state to be able to inflict comparatively limited damage on a major enemy: it would simply not be worth the major state's while to suffer it. There is a great deal of opposition to this view[2] and to the French *force de frappe* which, to some extent, embodies it. But quite apart from the specific validity of the theory for French purposes it does not seem entirely relevant to the case of the small state, *pace* General Gallois, as opposed to quondam world powers like France or Britain which are still great and powerful nations in any and every respect. As has already been noted, the small state, certainly one which is unaligned, is unlikely to constitute a major object of policy for a great power, *a fortiori* for a world power. It is in relation to some broader purpose that a major power is most apt to menace or attack a minor one. This may have the effect that General Gallois envisages, namely that where the minor state is possessed of sufficient nuisance value and determination, let alone strike

---

[1] Pierre Gallois, *Stratégie de l'âge nucléaire*, Paris, 1960.
[2] Of which the most effective is Raymond Aron, *Le Grand Débat*, Paris, 1963. See also Albert Wohlstetter, 'Nuclear Sharing: NATO and the N+1 Country', *Foreign Affairs*, April 1961.

capacity, it may avoid conflict altogether. But there may also be a contrary effect; and the fact that the small state relates to a broader target may operate in the opposite sense. The example of Belgium in 1914 is no less relevant than that of Switzerland after 1940. The prize sought by the Germans in 1914 was not Belgium but France. Had nuclear weapons been available at the time it is not entirely inconceivable that the Germans would have found substantial advantages in using them on Belgium as a means of deterring France and Britain from putting up effective resistance in their own defence, let alone in that of Belgium.

A further difficulty about the theory which relates the small state's strike capacity to its value as a prize is that, while an aggressor may believe it worth his while to exercise restraint in the case of a great industrial state the better to garner the economic, political and psychological benefits of its ultimate inclusion in his system, a minor state, being a smaller prize and therefore constituting a smaller increment may be, to that extent, expendable. Equally, for third powers the prospect that, say, France or Germany adhere to the Soviet system is of more consequence than if Switzerland or one of the Scandinavian states did and this must, in turn, affect their readiness to intervene. It follows that Sweden or Switzerland or any other small state which considers the acquisition of nuclear weapons as a reinforcement of its armoury for possible confrontation with a major nuclear power must plan for the most difficult of possible situations, one that strategically pits them against the greater state *alone*—even where the context of the conflict in political terms and ultimate purpose may be very much broader.

The key question is whether a policy for restricting the nuclear armoury to weapons suitable for tactical targets is likely to be successful where the enemy possesses, in addition to his own tactical weapons, an overwhelming strategic capability. Is it, in fact, reasonable to suppose that the advantages in the field (increased fire-power and the rest) can be had without the risk of encountering many or all of the dangers and horrors of counter-city nuclear warfare? (It must be remembered that the possibility of a small power acquiring a counter-*force* capability against a great nuclear power can be ruled out—certainly in the present state of the art and very probably forever.) Do nuclear weapons, in fact, offer the small power that extension of its military capacity in time and strength that it so badly needs?

The first thing to be noted is that the employment of nuclear weapons for tactical purposes is certain to ravage a very large area and that even if major centres of population are spared much of the country on both sides of the small state's border is likely to be laid waste. Nuclear attack on an invading force—except possibly a seaborne one—would in all probability lead to use of such weapons within the national territory. The dilemmas posed by a large drop of airborne forces would be particularly dreadful. Even if the great power's national territory were contiguous to that of the small, proportionately the latter would be likely to suffer substantially greater harm.

Secondly, the critical escalation at the present time is fairly obviously from conventional to nuclear weapons and not from one class of nuclear weapons to another. It may well be questioned whether the nominal threshold between tactical and strategic employment is, in all respects, a real one. There is no certainty that where the distinction between the two is held to by one side the fact will in all circumstances be immediately and unmistakably apparent to the commanders of the other. Nor is it probable that the decision to move from smaller to larger warheads and from tactical targets in the field to interdiction targets in the rear and from those to strategic targets proper will be weighed as carefully and taken as reluctantly as the decision to use nuclear weapons in the first place.

Finally, it is extremely difficult to believe that where a major nuclear power has had to face nuclear attack upon its forces—either in response to its own tactical employment of nuclear weapons or on the initiative of the defender—and has found the campaign going against it, that it will accept defeat or even a stalemate without employing, or at least threatening to employ, the greater force that is available to it. In short, the tactical use of nuclear weapons in the field seems unlikely to occur without many of the effects of strategic employment and without the strategic capability coming into play in one way or another.

It is true that a sparsely settled country like Sweden is better placed in this respect of the probable devastation of territory than a densely settled country like Switzerland. However, in a sparsely settled country, where both attacker and defender are obliged to disperse and the ratio of force to space is very low, the skilful attacker retains a considerable advantage which would probably outweigh the marginal benefit of presenting few strategic targets, or none at all.

It can be argued that such an escalation from tactical to strategic targets is not a *necessary* consequence of attack on the former and that the enemy will be governed by what he deems appropriate:

Un agresseur sans scrupules, ayant l'intention ferme de nous écraser par des bombardements atomiques massifs contre nos villes, le ferait sans d'abord prétexter que les forces suédoises sont susceptibles d'employer des armes atomiques contre l'envahisseur. Seuls ses propres calculs d'économie du combat influencerait son choix d'armes contre nous.[1]

But the principle of economy of means really relates to what is required for the object of the campaign to be secured. If the consequence of an initially successful defence by the attacked state is likely to be an overwhelming strategic onslaught by the invader, the leaders of the small state can hardly avoid asking themselves whether they dare risk resisting him and to what purpose.

The logic of this dilemma may appear to point in the direction of an extension of the nuclear armoury to include weapons of reprisal. If the capacity of the small state to harm

---

[1] General Westring, op. cit., p. 331.

the greater one is increased, reluctance to attack it, all other considerations being equal, will be greater. While the consequences of any form of nuclear war will be disastrous for the defender, the consequences for the attacker will vary with the nature and strength of the defender's armoury. And while the minor state is unlikely to acquire a counter-force capability or even a counter-city capability of sufficient quality and size to *guarantee* substantial harm to the enemy, the major power can never feel entirely immune and the possibility that even a single vehicle get past the defences must weigh with him. But such a widening of the possibilities would, it may be supposed, have three results. Firstly, it would mean that the likelihood of nuclear warfare entailing total or near-total destruction of the defending nation would be increased; secondly, the question of the employment of nuclear weapons of all categories would arise at a much earlier stage of the campaign, possibly even in a surprise attack; thirdly, the change in the character of the small power's military establishment could hardly fail to alter the framework of relations between the two states even in peace-time. It would, in fact, become a matter of high national policy for the great state, if it envisaged conflict as even a very remote possibility, to prevent the smaller state from acquiring such weapons and to coerce it into destroying them once they had been acquired. An instrument designed to support a defensive policy might thus be converted into a subject of conflict and help to precipitate the very confrontation which the small state must seek to avoid.

What, then, is left of the deterrent? Can it be effective; can it be, in the jargon, 'credible'? If the possession of nuclear weapons leaves the small power very nearly as vulnerable to nuclear blackmail as before even when it possesses a counter-city capability, and, in fact, every bit as vulnerable if its armoury is restricted to weapons largely or entirely suitable for tactical employment alone, what advantages has it gained by incurring the vast expense and concomitant dangers of acquiring them? If possession is a stimulus to nuclear warfare and nuclear warfare is likely to lead to the national territory being laid waste, while reprisal can mean, at most, a doubtful capacity to destroy a minor segment of the opponent's country, in what circumstances can the small power's leaders have good reason to take the decision to embark on such a programme in the first place? For, clearly, if it is to have any value and to make any kind of sense there must be some degree of assurance on *both* sides that there are, indeed, circumstances—at least in principle—when the weapons will be used.

It must be admitted that it is much easier to envisage circumstances in which nuclear weapons will not be used than ones in which they will be. It seems reasonable to suppose, for example, that possession of such weapons by both Czechs and Germans in 1938 would have stimulated the French and the British to yet greater efforts to dissuade the Czechs from resisting Germany and, at the same time, would have deepened the reluctance of the Czech Government to do so—if that were possible. In contrast, it is not inconceivable that had the Poles possessed such weapons in September 1939, they would have put them to use. Where the total destruction of the state and the captivity and ultimate annihilation of the people are in prospect the use of all available weapons has an undeniable validity and the apocalyptic urge to bring the temple walls crashing down upon one's enemies can appear the only proper course to a bruised and humiliated Samson. Would the Germans have attacked Czechoslovakia and Poland in the knowledge that they possessed nuclear weapons? Even without attempting an over-complex and inherently dubious extrapolation from contemporary strategic considerations to those of nearly three decades ago, it must be reckoned that in the Polish case they might well have done so and that the impending destruction of, say, Breslau and Koenigsberg would not have deterred Hitler, but only incited him to a greater frenzy of destruction in Poland itself. On the other hand, the case of Operation Green (against Czechoslovakia) might have gone differently and the opposition to Hitler in the German camp might have been more determined. The nerves and purposes of the attacker are of no less importance than those of the defender.

All of this would appear to illustrate and substantiate the essential point that the military consequences of the inequality of states persist into the nuclear age: only one side has to weigh the risks of overwhelming destruction. In one respect the inequality is intensified: given pre-nuclear arms alone a great power may defeat the regular forces of the small state and yet find itself bogged down in a long drawn out guerrilla war. Given nuclear arms and, of course, *the will to employ them* it can probably exclude that possibility.

In sum, it is hard to avoid the conclusion that, while a restricted number of highly industrialized small states have the scientific, technological and economic capacity to acquire an autonomous nuclear force, the deterrent value of such a capability is extremely limited. Faced with a major opponent its employment would in all probability signify destruction amounting to national suicide.

And yet there may be circumstances—rare but not inconceivable and for which there are historic precedents—where anything less than a nuclear capability would invite conquest while, given such a capability, the aggressor—in still rarer but still conceivable circumstances—might be deterred provided it was sufficiently clear to all concerned that the government in question was fully prepared to accept the risks and consequences of nuclear warfare. It would therefore follow that where a nuclear capability is acquired and maintained it can make sense provided it is seen as the retention of an option for such an event as, say, a resurgent and aggressive Germany or some radical (and at present inconceivable) change in Soviet policy and behaviour. However, since the establishment of a nuclear force is a very long-term process the question whether such—or similar—events are probable is perhaps less important than the belief that they are possible.[1]

III

The small state which pursues an active or aggressive policy in an under- or semi-developed environment is in a different case. The quality and destructive force of such nuclear weapons and weapon-systems as it can reasonably aspire to are very much more limited than in the case of the industrial state. The objects of its policy lie principally in the very different realm of relations with other small countries— not the major powers. The strategic and political implications of such an acquisition are, therefore, likely to be very different.[2]

The question of nuclear weapons designed for tactical use hardly arises. They are substantially more difficult and costly to produce,[3] requiring a very high degree of technological and industrial skill. A less sophisticated and less accurate weapon may be extremely effective against major centres of population, and yet useless or even dangerous to employ against armoured forces, fortifications and the like in view of the twin dangers that the targets would escape harm while one's own forces would not. Fission warheads designed for tactical use require much the same quantities of plutonium as those for counter-city attack. The total quantity of plutonium available to such a state is unlikely to be great—

---

[1] It is of interest that Swedish defence plans appear to be geared to the retention of a nuclear option without the commitment to take it up. Research is pursued without production (so far as is known) and General Rapp, the Swedish Commander-in-Chief, is reported to have expressed the view that a tactical weapon in the 1–20 kiloton range could be produced and deployed within three years of the decision to do so, or in a shorter period if the necessary research effort were made in good time. (*Aviation Week*, 5 July 1965.) Furthermore, it is 'an open secret' that the Viggen jet-fighter has been designed to carry nuclear weapons, if necessary. (*Guardian*, 13 October 1964.)

[2] The present topic is, of course, entirely speculative, possibly unreal. No state in this category appears, at the time of writing, to have a capacity for autonomous production of nuclear weapons and the probability of such weapons being supplied by major powers is so remote as to be hardly worth discussing—for the reasons, among others, that were mentioned at the beginning of this chapter.

[3] The 'Sergeant' tactical missile cost the United States $500 million to develop. (Neville Brown, op. cit., p. 199.)

perhaps no more than can be produced at the rate of one or two warheads a year and quite possibly less. Limited productive capacity may itself be a disincentive to produce weapons for tactical use. It is also doubtful whether a small underdeveloped state would offer tactical targets of sufficient importance to justify the employment of nuclear weapons against them, except, possibly, interdiction targets such as harbours and major airfields. And these may be indistinguishable in practice from attacks on population. Finally, the limited number of weapons would tend to rule out a counter-force strategy, even if the delivery systems were sufficiently accurate for such purposes. It follows that rational use of such limited nuclear power may be thought to imply attack on cities.

Where the enemy is similarly armed it will be clear that any nuclear attack is likely to be followed by reprisal with all weapons available to the defender. For given a small absolute number of weapons there will be no military advantage in limiting the reprisal; the attacker will very likely have exhaused his own supply in the first strike. Alternatively, if there is reason to believe that he has not used all his arsenal in the first strike safety (quite apart from vengeance) will lie in an attempt to destroy the enemy's centres of population and government in the hope of shattering his command structure. There will be very little to be gained from restraint. Once this is recognized by the prospective attacker, he himself will have every incentive to strike very hard initially, *if at all*. The question of an 'acceptable' degree of damage hardly arises in the case of a state with a small population and two or three major centres of industry and population which are themselves the only rational strategic targets and therefore probably doomed in the event of nuclear exchange, no matter how brief or how limited in intensity.[1]

---

[1] The preceding argument may be expanded as follows. A small, Afro-Asian nuclear power could not be expected to acquire (ten or fifteen years after the initial decision to go nuclear) significantly more than, say, a wing of (perhaps twelve) suitably equipped aircraft or relatively unsophisticated missiles and a like number

Nuclear warfare between two small, semi-developed powers would thus seem likely to be even more senseless—if that were possible—than between more powerful states. Damage to the civilian centres would be immense, but the quality and numbers of the weapons would probably be insufficient to ensure commensurate damage to the military forces on the ground. If the military command structures emerged unharmed once the small nuclear arsenals had been exhausted, conventional forces could still operate in the field. If this were so, the most important elements of such societies would remain substantially intact, which is the opposite of what is required.

The small power which is resolved on an active strategy can, in fact, hope to attain its object more effectively and with far less danger of incurring interference and intervention from the outside and harm to itself by employing indirect and subversive instruments of policy. So long as such means can be employed with relative impunity against the soft targets for which they are suited—states with fragile régimes and heterogeneous populations—military measures of any kind, and nuclear warfare doubly so, would be inappropriate. Where the target states are unlikely to acquire

of plutonium bombs in the twenty kiloton range, or less. For a strategic, essentially counter-city strike this would not be inappropriate. There are few such states with more than two or three really large urban centres; many have only one. On the other hand, if the attacking state, State A, is to retain a counter-city capability it can hardly risk a counter-force strike unless the attacked state, State B, keeps his aircraft in the vicinity of its cities, which is unlikely. State B, moreover, can deploy its own nuclear force in widely separated fields and increase the number of targets it presents to A. It can do so more easily and rapidly than A can increase the number of its weapons. Finally, if pilot error, faulty intelligence and, above all, ultimate failure to penetrate B's defences completely are all taken into account, it may be seen that A's small nuclear force cannot be relied on to execute a fully successful counter-force strike against B, regardless of whether or not A insists on retaining a counter-city capability. A must consider the high probability that some element of B's nuclear force remains in being and capable of operating in a second strike. But B will be aware that a strong effort by A to reduce its own nuclear force would very seriously weaken and perhaps exhaust A's capacity to attack B's cities. In consequence, B will have a powerful incentive to retaliate directly against the aggressor's centres of population whether or not its own centres had suffered attack. Once this were realized by A, the plan to attack B's forces before all else would lose much of its validity.

a nuclear capability, being for the most part at the bottom of the scale of industrial and scientific potential, the prospect of facing a nuclear threat by a powerful neighbour might well impel them to search for ways of associating themselves with extra-regional powers able to guarantee their integrity. If this occurred the net effect of the aggressive state's move into the nuclear class would be to impede its own progress. Alternatively, the states which felt threatened might attempt to alter the political relations subsisting between them and proceed to forms of federation and alliance that would isolate the aggressive state and remove many of the advantages that lay in being the strongest of a group of divided equals. It may be supposed, for example, that had President Nkrumah in his heyday sought to acquire nuclear weapons the fear and resentment which he inspired even without them in many African states would have greatly increased and led to political and military consequences which would have done nothing to facilitate the execution of his policy. And lastly, the great advantage of subversion as a political weapon—the fact that it attacks authority with the help of elements of the population which is subject to it—would be lost once it was replaced or reinforced by a weapon which attacks the population directly and the government only by extension.

The example of the Chaco War in which two under-developed states engaged in protracted and disastrous warfare[1] with only the minimum of interference (and even some encouragement[2]) from other powers suggests that such an event cannot be totally ruled out and that it cannot be taken as axiomatic that third parties will intervene. But there are reasons for thinking it improbable. All nuclear powers, but first and foremost the major ones, have an interest in preserving the present, generalized inhibition against the use of nuclear weapons. There is nothing to be gained by breaking

[1] The casualties and cost were 3½ per cent. of the population and $124·5 million for Paraguay and 2 per cent. of the population and $228 million for Bolivia. Zook, op. cit., p. 240.
[2] Cf. Chapter 5, p. 108.

the pattern and, in all probability, a great deal to be lost. The heavy pressures against proliferation which may be impending are likely to be directed in their most intense form against states pursuing an active strategy—or faced with one—not merely because they are highly vulnerable to coercion by major powers on other grounds, but because, unlike those which were discussed in the previous section of the present chapter, their acquisition of nuclear weapons will not provide the compensating satisfaction for one world bloc that, in practical terms, the new nuclear force is designed to deter the other, complicating rather than simplifying its strategic considerations and military dispositions. In so far as there can be a concerted effort on the part of the great powers to prevent the proliferation of nuclear weapons among the minor ones, it is here that it is most likely to be effective and straightforward.

In the light of these strategic and political considerations it is hard to see what advantage a small state bent on pursuing an active strategy can derive from a nuclear capability, except, perhaps, for a limited increment to its prestige. Of course, if prestige is valued more highly than substantive power—which may be the case, though not as frequently as some suppose—then the attempt may be made despite the regional and international consequences of the acquisition of such weapons.

However, where it is the conflict of the aggressive small state with major powers that is in question and it is against one of them that the weapons are, or may be, directed, then a very different set of considerations will surely operate on all sides. It is, for example, hard to believe that the Anglo-French landing in Egypt would have taken place or the attack taken the form it did had Egypt possessed even a small nuclear force at the time. But in such an event the *raison d'être* of an Egyptian nuclear force would have been deterrence, not aggression. The strategic situation would then have been on all fours with that which was discussed earlier in this chapter, namely one which obtains when a small nuclear power confronts a major one, the only material difference being that the dangers and difficulties which must be ascribed even to a highly developed small state with a relatively sophisticated and effective nuclear force and a command and control system of commensurate quality would have been multiplied many times over where weapons and delivery systems were of poorer and less reliable quality.

IV

If a nuclear force is to be of any value to a small state it is as a deterrent to major opposition. Yet even as a deterrent it is, as has been suggested, of uncertain value; and the circumstances in which it might be employed are difficult to envisage, if not improbable—doubly so if the force is limited to weapons suitable for tactical purposes alone. In contrast, the decision to *abstain* from acquiring nuclear weapons has reasonably clear implications. It renders the state in question vulnerable to nuclear blackmail and makes both the deterrent and active efficacy of the conventional defence establishment dependent on the inhibitions of the hostile power concerning employment of nuclear weapons on the one hand and the contingent strategic considerations of other nuclear powers which are not parties to the conflict on the other. But faced with such a situation the latter, however friendly, will first look to their own security and resolve on their response as best they understand their own interests. This means, in effect, that the question whether the conventionally armed small state's defence establishment will play any role at all in the event of conflict with a nuclear power will be determined as much by the major powers as a group—whether or not they are in conflict with the state—as by its own civil and military leaders.

The employment of a conventional defence establishment in case of conflict with a major, nuclear power is thus founded for the small state on a logic that differs only slightly from that which underlies the employment by it of nuclear weapons. In either case the purpose is to provide the

state's leaders with as good a hand and as varied a set of
options as possible, while yet leaving them with the ultimate
option of resolving not to play at all. A greater degree of
certainty can only be found in the decision to retain fewer
options: to disarm conventionally at one level, to abstain
from nuclear armament at another.

There is, indeed, a wide range of possibilities and options
beginning with total military incapacity or absolute abstention from exploiting whatever capacity exists and ending
with tactical and strategic nuclear capabilities. At one end
of the range reliance on the aid and support—or indifference—of other, greater powers is total. At the other end it
is minimal, yet still very great. However, while a rise in the
scale provides a greater number of military options, it, at
the same time, increases the dangers of putting what might
be termed the marginal one to practical effect. For this
reason the political consequence of acquiring a substantially
wider range of weapons may well be increasing stultifica-
tion. Instead of enhancing the net power and influence of
small states, the acquisition of a nuclear capability is likely
to narrow their field of political manœuvre and intensify
their sensitivity to pressure. Certainly, it will further inhibit
them from taking political initiatives and encourage them to
abstain from any move that might embroil them in conflict.
For the state intent on a defensive policy this, in itself, may
not be thought a high price to pay. For the state which
pursues an active or aggressive policy the effect may be
capital. If it is the political consequences of nuclear proliferation that some of the major powers fear, their fears seem
unfounded.

Nevertheless, the opposition of the great powers (with the
possible exception of China) to the proliferation of nuclear
weapons remains very great and minor candidates for
membership in the nuclear club must take it to heart and
into account. The weaker they are, the more isolated, and
the greater their economic and strategic vulnerability to
coercion by the major powers the more serious the political

and other consequences of acquiring a nuclear capability
are likely to be. These, coupled to the somewhat uncertain
but evidently grave strategic implications of such a capability
in the event of conflict have sufficed, thus far, to deter any
minor power from going beyond the intermediate stage of
taking out the scientific and technological options, while
leaving the decision to produce weapons for a later stage—
one which may well be postponed indefinitely. However,
since the significance of being in a position (comparable to
that of India today) where it is within the power of the state
to acquire weapons within a relatively brief period of time
will be thoroughly understood by all who would be concerned in the event that weapons were actually acquired, a
government so placed is potentially as great a target for
pressure and intimidation as one that has gone the full
distance. And since, in practice, it appears to be extremely
difficult to disguise the existence of the substantial scientific
and industrial plant that is the precondition of even such an
intermediate stage, the possibility of advancing from conventional to nuclear armament without enduring a period of
time when the state will be obliged to bear consequences
comparable to those entailed by possession of the weapons
without such small advantages as actual possession would
bring in their wake seems extremely remote.

Given this range of possibilities the point at which a state
will come to rest will naturally depend, in the first instance,
on its economic and human potential. But at the margin, the
point will be determined by the broad views held by its
leaders of the country's needs, of the international role to
which it is best suited and, above all, of the degree to which
concomitant risks and danger can be justified in terms of the
effort to retain effective independence of policy. What seems
clear is that there must be some correlation between a
rational decision to opt for nuclear weapons and the value—
irrational as are all value judgements—attached to the political
independence of the state. It may be supposed that where
the implications of such a correlation are clear to all and the

possible practical consequences of such a decision are understood and feared, the attachment to political independence may weaken. Indeed, the tenuous character of the political independence of small states and the force of the pressures impelling them to rely on and, ultimately, align themselves with great powers are perhaps nowhere so clearly exposed as in this context of the two questions: which among the small states can acquire nuclear weapons and what strategic advantages can those which are real candidates for them hope to obtain?

economic, military and organizational resources would soon
be felt. Moreover, these disparities could be brought to bear
by the stronger party on the weaker long before the conflict
emerged into the public light, to say nothing of its assuming
violent form. In brief, the cornerstone of any Central
American republic's foreign policy is its relations with the
United States—as Guatemala's conflict with the United
States in the early fifties and Cuba's today so amply
illustrate. Whether, in such circumstances, these and other
small states which are similarly placed can be described as
fully sovereign and politically independent is largely a matter of definition and opinion. But it is worth noting that the
conventions of sovereignty and legal equality and of inter-
international behaviour generally are such that it remains
possible, even for a small client state, to rebel against the
paramount power without violating international practice
and habits of thought and, possibly, with some prospect of
receiving support from other major states. The ability *in
principle* to alter course and reconsider political and economic
arrangements entered into in past times is a fair test of
political independence at an elementary level. The capacity
to carry out such a decision in the face of opposition is a test
of political independence at a second level, a more important one. It is at this latter level that the viability of the state
is tested, i.e. by its capacity to withstand opposition and stick
to purposes thought commensurate with the national interest. But whereas the great powers are, ultimately, impervious
to coercion, the degree of opposition that small states can
reasonably be expected to withstand will vary from case to
case and be amenable, in the final analysis, only to subjective
evaluation. Viability, in consequence, is a relative quality
fluctuating with circumstances, possessed by different states
in a different degree, but in no case absolutely and finally as
it is by the major powers. Furthermore, where the opposition
is very great and the capacity of the state to overcome it is
doubtful, it is the national interest itself that must be reconsidered. It may lie, quite simply, in passivity—a condi-

10

CONCLUSIONS

THE general question with which this study has been concerned is whether a small and independent state is viable in
the world of contemporary international politics and to what
degree and under what circumstances. It is clear that there
are, in practice, a number of states in this category whose
viability is not in question at the present time because they
are spared having to sustain any serious opposition to their
purposes—including the fundamental one of political survival. Yet for that reason little of general significance about
the small states as a class can be learnt from examining their
affairs. The question whether, say, El Salvador is inter-
nationally viable cannot be divorced from the fortunate circumstance that its external relations present it with few
problems of any gravity. It is under no military threat; it
chooses not to oppose the paramount power in Central
America in any of the latter's major purposes; and it is
assured of that power's support should it find itself under
threat from either its neighbours or another major power.
There is thus no apparent, *structural* reason why it should not
maintain its political identity for as far as the prophetic eye
can see. Of course, the tranquillity of El Salvador's external
affairs is conditional upon the pursuit of what might be
termed a non-policy, one of passivity in the international
arena. Should the United States require something of the
El Salvador Government that the latter finds excessively
disagreeable or should El Salvador itself embark on a
political course which the United States, for its part,
finds discordant with its policy for the region the material
inequality between the two states, the vast disparity in

tion in which most small states are placed, some by choice, some by dint of circumstances and others (many of the new states in Africa, for example) because, while they have been spared the full blast of major opposition thus far, they are still chiefly concerned with internal affairs. To dismiss all these—the majority of the members of the class that has been discussed here—as states that are sovereign only in form and not in any of the real implications of the term would be absurd. They retain important options, of which the greatest, as has been said, is that of changing course. But because of their present passivity it is impossible to say how they would fare except by analogy with the cases of those states which, given roughly equivalent resources, have ventured further. It is therefore on the Guatemalas— and Finlands and Hungarys—of the world that this study has dwelt and also on those, such as Cambodia, Egypt, Ghana, Guinea and Israel, which face heavy opposition from lesser powers, but which have this in common with those directly confronted by the great states that they are alone and must rely, in the last resort, on their own political and material resources. By analogy and by extension, such cases are instructive even for states, such as Australia and Malaysia, which at present have the benefit of the political encouragement and material support of the great powers, but which need to consider how far they can, in fact, manage on their own in the event of such support slackening or lapsing totally.

On the whole, the picture that emerges is a sombre one. The price of independence and effective sovereignty at the second level mentioned here may be extremely heavy both in human and material terms. Where the external opposition is very great it may be quite beyond the power of the small state to withstand it even where it is both socially and economically feasible for the government in question to lead its subjects to heavy and unusual sacrifices and exertions. At the same time, since it is the combination of physical resources with human determination that matters in any given case it is impossible to say flatly where the breaking point may be. The imponderables are at least as important as those resources which are measurable in terms of arms, supplies, money and manpower.

What does seem clear is that the price is rising and that the effort that is required of governments and peoples is likely to increase with time rather than diminish. And further, that the condition of ultimate reliance on autonomous strength—which for the sake of brevity has been termed non-alignment throughout this study—is one which increases and multiplies the difficulties that are common to all small states regardless of the character of their relations with others.

Yet it does not therefore follow that the small and unaligned state is an anachronism in the sense that the struggle to maintain political autonomy with meagre resources is one which cannot be maintained in the contemporary world, nor that the somewhat patronizing and impatient view held of small states by leaders, officials and many scholars of great nations is essentially a true one. Admittedly, it is easy to fit the pattern of spiralling difficulties which has been described here into the larger, familiar notion that there is, generally, a trend away from the independent state towards larger units and that these alone are truly viable. Thus Lester Pearson:

> In this new era on which we have entered, the effective unit of foreign policy and strategy is no longer the nation state, however large, but the coalition of such states brought together and held together for certain purposes.[1]

But in fact this view, however agreeable to contemplate, is open to serious objections. The weight of recent evidence is all to the effect that the coalition or alliance is not an effective unit of foreign policy and strategy at all, except in the narrow, if extremely important, respect that it can from time to time marshal great strength. So long as it is a true *coalition*

[1] Lester Pearson, *Democracy in World Politics*, Princeton, 1956, p. 40.

of equal partners it is unwieldy and subject to the weakness that apart from the 'certain purposes' which hold it together there are almost invariably other purposes which are held separately and which are mutually incompatible. In consequence, a coalition requires collective leadership and the sinking of national interests as individually defined by each member. In war-time and in great international crises this may be acceptable. In other periods leadership is likely to lapse into domination by the senior partner and the willing sinking of interests be replaced by resentment and resistance. No two states are alike and no two states can arrive at an identical appreciation of their national interest. Unless the coalition is replaced by a *confederation*, that is, unless the political and institutional relations that subsist between the member states and between each one of the member states and other states which are external to the system are thoroughly re-ordered, the coalition is unlikely to survive the crisis in which it was born for very long. At all events, the attempt to keep it in being beyond the point where interests seriously diverge can be disastrous for the state which is obliged to make the major concessions. And it is, of course, the small state which is called upon to make sacrifices, as Munich illustrates in classic manner. It would therefore be misleading to argue that the solution to the small state's problems lies in alliance and other forms of semi-permanent association with more powerful states without taking these dangers into account—unless, indeed, the association or coalition is intended as no more than a stage preliminary to full integration. Naturally, if the small state loses its political identity by merger with other states its problems as such are solved. It may be that as a *programme* the amalgamation of states has a great deal to recommend it, even though the difficulties in the way of its execution are only too familiar. But this is a question of a different order and certainly one that is beyond the bounds of a study that is concerned with the *de facto* world of states.

But over and above the question of a voluntary or

involuntary change in the contemporary state system the temptation to argue from the difficulties that beset the small state to the proposition that it is an anachronism is only justified if states so placed have a reasonably free choice to make. In fact, only a few have one. Non-alignment is by no means exclusively a political posture, freely adopted because of its international uses. In many cases it is as much a symptom of the situation in which the state finds itself as a recipe for dealing with it. For Cambodia, Finland and Israel, for example, there is no alternative today to their admittedly precarious condition of non-alignment because the only states with which they can conceivably merge or even ally themselves with are either those with which they are in conflict or are states which demonstrably have nothing to gain by such a merger and a great deal to lose. Where non-alignment is a consequence of conflict and the conflict itself is due to a fundamental incompatibility between states and societies, abandonment of sovereignty would mean the sacrifice of social and national issues of the first importance. Once again, certainty would only be purchased at very heavy cost, probably heavier than that which must be borne in the effort to maintain independence. It is natural that it be rejected.

For yet another group, those unaligned states which pursue an aggressive or active policy, merger on a basis of equality may be possible, but it would mean a radical change in the political purposes of the state and resignation to the prospect of a transfer of domestic power. Neither of these are likely to be acceptable to the ambitious, power-hungry leaders who are so often an essential element of the driving force behind an aggressive national policy.

All these appear valid reasons for thinking that there is very little prospect of the small and politically autarchic states with which most of the continents are studded gently withering away by dissolving into larger units as a straightforward consequence of the difficulties and disabilities inherent in their situation. Some may succumb in time, but other small states, disappointed in the coalitions of which they are now members, may choose a propitious moment to escape from the orbit of a great power and take the place of those who could not stay the course.

Broadly speaking, it would seem that the contradictions between the pursuit of political independence and national security on the one hand and the consequences of limited human and material resources on the other can only be resolved in two ways. One is by a fall in the value attached to political independence and to the nation state as such; the other is by the great powers applying overwhelming force against their weaker, isolated opponents. There are no signs of this occurring in the near future, but it is not impossible or even difficult to envisage.

The implications of the acquisition of nuclear power—if thought out to the end—come close to indicating limits to which the impulsion to maintain and fortify national independence can reasonably be allowed to lead. From recognition of these limits doubts about the logic which impls states to approach them may gradually emerge. This may well be true of all states, irrespective of size, but, as in so many other aspects of national power, the implications of nuclear warfare are harshest for the small nation. To that extent critical re-thinking of the moral and ideological bases of political nationalism is likely to carry more weight and to be informed by greater urgency in a small community than in a large one.

Whether the great powers will ever again proceed to employ the tremendous force that is available to them to the full is a great question in itself, well beyond the scope of this study. But it is a question which is reasonable to ask, even though no clear answer is now apparent. The inhibitions to which the great states are subject at the present time derive, in the first instance, from the strategic and political relationship which has arisen between them in the last two decades, though the broad political philosophies of those who lead the powers and residual memories of the Second World

War are also factors of no small relevance and importance. However, should the character and purposes of great power leaders change and should the emergence of China as a major nuclear power alter this strategic relationship very substantially, as indeed it might, it is not impossible that the behaviour of the United States and the Soviet Union towards third parties may acquire an asperity that, up to now, has been reserved for special problems such as those of Cuba and Hungary. Equally, if the United States were to withdraw its presence from South East Asia it is likely that the character of the relations between China and the many small states on its periphery will change and that the full implications of the latter's weakness and exposure to China's great strength be felt very rapidly.

All in all, a clear appreciation of the small states' condition is made difficult by the fortunate circumstance that the great powers operate today in a climate of thought which promotes caution and hesitation, particularly where the use of force is in question. This too may change. The conception of what is politically permissible and what can safely be done by one great power without fear of retaliation or counter-action by another, or, indeed, any significant reaction at all, may alter. The practice of pursuing great-power rivalry through minor intermediaries so as to avoid direct confrontation between the major states may take on new forms. Russia might respond to the arming of West Germany with nuclear weapons by the occupation of Finland, or even Sweden. A really effective penetration of Africa or the Middle East by China might impel both Russia and America to abandon all restraint in their dealings with those regions, imposing rigid spheres of influence and tight control of regional affairs. There is no reason not to take such possibilities into account.

The survival of small, politically isolated states as independent powers is thus precarious, depending on a multitude of factors over many of which they themselves have little influence. Long-term considerations in all major fields—

the economic, the military and the political—are disquiet-ing. And yet, what has been said of the economic sphere is largely true of the political and military: in an imperfect world a great many short- and middle-term tactics can be adopted to keep the machinery of state running and to keep a measure of autonomous control over the national destiny. Some states will be more successful in this than others, either because they are better placed in terms of resources or else because they are more fortunate in their opponents. Still, the crucial factor in almost every case is the human one and where the society coheres and is strongly led very great obstacles can often be overcome. This, at any rate, is the evidence of the past. So although it is fairly plain that sur-vival will require an ever increasing effort, it is unlikely that the effort be lightly abandoned, at any rate by strong societies, until an entirely unassailable obstacle has actually been reached. And for some that may not occur for a very considerable period.

SELECT BIBLIOGRAPHY

Books and Official Publication

Aron Raymond, *Le Grand Débat*, Paris, 1963.
Australian Institute of Political Science, *Australia's Defence and Foreign Policy*, Melbourne, 1964.
Barbey, B., *P.C. du Général*, Neuchâtel, 1948.
Beneš, Edvard, *Memoirs*, London, 1954.
Blackstock, Paul W., *The Strategy of Subversion*, Chicago, 1964.
Buchan, Alastair, (Ed.), *A World of Nuclear Powers?*, Englewood Cliffs, 1966.
Correa, H., *The Economics of Human Resources*, Amsterdam, 1963.
Coward, H. Roberts, *Military Technology in Developing Countries*, Cambridge, Mass., 1964.
Ernst, Fritz, *European Switzerland*, Zürich, 1951.
Fanon, Frantz, *The Wretched of the Earth*, London, 1965.
Foot, M. R. D., *Men in Uniform*, London, 1961.
Fox, Annette Baker, *The Power of Small States, Diplomacy in World War II*, Chicago, 1959.
Gallois, Pierre, *Stratégie de l'Âge nucléaire*, Paris, 1960.
Giap, Vo Nguyen, *People's War People's Army*, Hanoi, 1961.
Hindmarsh, Albert E., *Force in Peace*, Cambridge, Mass., 1933.
Hitch, Charles J., and McKean, Roland N., *The Economics of Defense in the Nuclear Age*, Cambridge, Mass., 1960.
Hussein, (King), *Uneasy Lies the Head*, London, 1962.
Jakobson, Max, *The Diplomacy of the Winter War*, Cambridge, Mass., 1961.
Kimche, Jon, *Spying for Peace; General Guisan and Swiss Neutrality*, 1961.
Knorr, Klaus, *The War Potential of Nations*, Princeton, 1956.
Ledermann, Laszlo, *Considérations sur le Petit État*, Neuchâtel, 1946.
Lederrey, Ernst, *Importance Stratégique de la Suisse des origines à l'ère atomique*, Lausanne, 1959.
Lyon, Peter, *Neutralism*, Leicester, 1963.
Macartney, C. A., *October Fifteenth*, Edinburgh, 1956.
Mannerheim, Marshal G. C., *Memoirs*, London, 1953.
Mao Tse-tung and Guevara, Ernesto ('Che'), *Guerilla Warfare*, London, 1963.
Michaely, Michael, *Concentration in International Trade*, Amsterdam, 1962.
Mosley, Leonard, *Haile Selassie*, London, 1964.

Namier, L. B., *The Case for Bohemia*, London, 1917.
Örvik, Nils, *The Decline of Neutrality*, 1914–41, Oslo, 1953.
Perkins, Dexter, *A History of the Monroe Doctrine*, London, 1960.
Robinson, E. A. G. (Ed.), *Economic Consequences of the Size of Nations*, London, 1963.
Royal Institute of International Affairs, *International Sanctions*, London, 1938.
——*Survey of International Affairs*, *1939–46*, *The War and the Neutrals*, London, 1956.
Schneider, Ronald M., *Communism in Guatemala*, 1944–54, New York, 1959.
Seale, Patrick, *The Struggle for Syria*, London, 1965.
Smith, Roger M., *Cambodia's Foreign Policy*, Ithaca, 1965.
Spence, J. E., *Republic Under Pressure*, London, 1965.
Tanner, Väinö, *The Winter War*, Stanford, 1957.
Tingsten, Herbert, *The Debate on the Foreign Policy of Sweden*, London, 1949.
Touval, Saadia, *Somali Nationalism*, Cambridge, Mass., 1963.
Trinquier, Roger, *La Guerre Moderne*, Paris, 1961.
United Nations, *Towards a Dynamic Development Policy for Latin America*, New York, 1963.
Upton, Anthony F., *Finland in Crisis*, *1940–41*, London, 1964.
Vandenbosch, Amry, *Dutch Foreign Policy since 1815*, The Hague, 1959.
Wilson, David A., *Politics in Thailand*, Ithaca, 1962.
Young, George K., *Masters of Indecision*, London, 1962.
Zook, David H., *The Conduct of the Chaco War*, New Haven, 1960.

Articles

Aebi, U., and others, 'La Suisse et son équipement en armes atomiques', Societé d'études militaires, *Evolution de l'Armée suisse*, *Documentation*, Cahier No. 11, 1962.
Beneš, Edvard, 'Why Czechoslovakia did not fight', *Central European Observer*, 17 January 1941.
Cecil, Charles O., 'The Determinants of Libyan Foreign Policy', *Middle East Journal*, Winter, 1965.
Codding, George A., 'The New Swiss Military Capability', *Foreign Affairs*, April 1962.
Fisher, H. A. L., 'The Value of Small States', *Studies in History and Politics*, London, 1920.
Gordon, Bernard, 'Cambodia: Where Foreign Policy Counts', *Asian Survey*, September 1965.
Grandchamp, René, 'Finlande, Scandinavie, U.R.S.S. et O.T.A.N.', *Revue de Défense Nationale*, December 1960.

Holsti, Kalevi J., 'Strategy and Techniques of Influence in Soviet-Finnish Relations, *Western Political Quarterly*, March 1964.

Kroef, Justus M. van der, 'The West New Guinea Settlement: its Origins and Implications', *Orbis*, Spring 1963.

Mark, W., 'Armes atomiques pour l'armée suisse—Pouvoir ou Vouloir?', *Revue Militaire Suisse*, December 1963.

Paltridge, Shane, 'Australia and the Defence of Southeast Asia', *Foreign Affairs*, October 1965.

Pickert, General, 'The Value of Numbers in the Nuclear Age', *Survival*, September–October 1961.

Schaffer, B. B., 'Policy and System in Defense: The Australian Case', *World Politics*, January 1963.

Schwartz, Urs, 'Country Problems: Switzerland', *Disarmament and Arms Control*, Winter, 1963–4.

Tingsten, Herbert, 'Issues in Swedish Foreign Policy', *Foreign Affairs*, April 1959.

Vital, David, 'Czechoslovakia and the Powers, September 1938', *Journal of Contemporary History*, October 1966.

Westring, Adolph, 'Le problème des armes atomiques en Suède', *Revue Militaire Générale*, March 1958.

Wiskemann, Elizabeth, 'The state of Switzerland in 1956', *International Affairs*, October 1956.

Wohlstetter, Albert, 'Nuclear Sharing: N.A.T.O. and the N+1 Country', *Foreign Affairs*, April 1961.

Wuorinen, John H., 'Finland and the U.S.S.R.—1945–61', *Journal of International Affairs*, No. 1, xvi, 1962.

Zartman, I. William, 'Neutralism and Neutrality in Scandinavia', *Western Political Quarterly*, June 1954.

INDEX

DATE DUE

GAYLORD

PRINTED IN U.S.A.